It's Not Over Yet

Thoughts and Tales of One Woman's Journey

MONA PEARL

FEDORA PRESS

FIRST EDITION

Cover & Interior Design by Scribe Freelance | www.scribefreelance.com

Learn more about the author or this publication at: www.fedorapress.com

ISBN: 978-1-936712-06-9

Published in the United States of America

I dedicate this book . . . my legacy . . .
In memory of:

My parents, Hilda and Bill Marks
and

My beloved husband, David
and

My departed brother, Dr. Myles Marks
and
For my children

Clifford, Todd, and Tina
and
For my grandchildren

Alison, Joshua, Alexander, and Bradley
How Blesssed I Am . . .

I Love You Now and Forever

The mind is the helm of the ship we steer throughout our lifetime.

Navigate with your heart and soul.

Steady as she goes!

—MONA PEARL

CONTENTS

Introduction

Today is the day I set out to change the direction of my life. Will I encounter more hurdles? Probably . . . but I'm learning to jump higher.

I AM A STORYTELLER who writes—not a writer who tells a story.

Within this book I wish to share some of the thoughts and tales of my life. My hope is that you will recognize yourself somewhere among these pages, and know that you are not alone.

Having travelled to many places in this world, I realize how connected we are. I visited five Eastern-Bloc countries before the fall of Communism. If there is anything I learned from my travels, it is that people are basically the same—only the culture, the language and traditions are different. Realizing that connection opened my heart, mind and soul to the acceptance, understanding and appreciation of all people.

I worked for several years as a fashion model, but have never been a career woman. Marrying a man whose mother was a powerful, career woman, my husband desired a wife who remained at home.

Many women of my generation were stay-at-home moms, although among my friends and acquaintances some were teachers, one was an interior designer and another was a librarian. Most of my close friends remained at home, for various reasons. We were the women who worked for charities, carpooled the children to after-school activities and had dinner and a cocktail ready for our husbands when they returned home from a stressful day at work.

I became a "career" wife and mother, raising my three children. Gifting the world with loving, caring and altruistic children has been my most gratifying accomplishment.

But, remaining an at-home mom also gave me the opportunity to pursue and enjoy so many pastimes. I knew I had a gift for some of them. I studied painting, singing and writing, and was involved in charity work. Having been a fashion design major in college, and having married a man in the fashion business, I also enjoyed sharing my fashion ability with my husband while he was on business trips.

I have been scribbling my thoughts on napkins, torn-out pages from puzzle books and scraps of paper in my handbag and writing stories from the mundane to the miraculous for most of my life.

I delighted in telling stories for children of all ages. At the request of my eight-year-old grandson, some of my stories were read to his class. The principal then asked me for more, as the children had enjoyed them. A friend, a schoolteacher, also read some of my stories to her class. One of her students, a little imp, ran off with one of the originals.

Heartache and tragedy are lessons for life, but with hope, faith and wisdom, we can create joy, peace and fulfillment. There will always be the good times and the bad times. I've learned that humor is an important ingredient in balancing the equation of life. My love of humor induced me to add a few of my thoughts and tales of humor throughout the "journey" in my book.

I've shared in this book many of the joys of my life, but have excluded more of the heartaches. If I placed joys and heartaches in "column A" and "column B," then totaled them, I would still consider myself a winner. I have been blessed.

One cannot always appreciate the good unless one has experienced the opposite. It often takes the greatest losses in life to learn the greatest lessons. I've learned to appreciate everything, for these are the lessons of life.

It is time to review my life. Where have I been and where am I going?

I often wonder, have I lived another life? Why do places I've never been to feel so familiar—and faces I see and people I meet, I sometimes sense I've known before? I live in the here and now, not in the past.

In so many ways, we all share the joy, the pain, the emptiness and the fulfillment of life.

Three-quarters of a century of living have passed. Some of you will relate to my own experiences and others will not. But, all will understand the emotions of human existence. The experiences need not be the same, but the same feelings run through each of us like a river.

The inclusion of the many photographs in this book adds a dimension to the expression, "A picture speaks a thousand words."

Now that I am in the twilight of my years, I look back, and I've come to the realization that the *coming-of-age* appears much later in life.

And here I am . . .

Acknowledgments

WHERE DO I BEGIN to say thank you for giving me the ingredients for the stories that I share with you in this book?

I must begin with my parents, who raised me with unconditional love and gave me the greatest sense of self, without creating an egotist.

My husband, David, who believed in my ability to write and always encouraged me to express this gift I was given.

My children, Cliff, Todd and Tina, who, just by their existence, supplied so much of the material that enabled me to write.

My grandchildren, Ali, Alex, Josh and Brad, who kept me on my toes. I loved telling them stories when they were growing up, and this encouraged me to pen many of those short stories.

I must thank Lewis Frumkes, my mentor. Lewis is head of the Writing Center at Hunter College. Many years ago, Lewis told me I was a true storyteller, and he urged me to continue to write.

And to Lewis' wife, Alana, I thank you for your brilliant editing skills.

Big THANK YOUS go to CiCi, for believing in me. Your encouragement in the continuing process of streamlining my book was a major incentive for me. Daniel . . . you are the best. As an artistic director, responsible for the beautiful cover of my book and putting it all together, you kept me focused and inspired. Thank you.

Last, but most important, I owe a very big thank you to my very dear friend, Linda Brody. Linda carefully perused every written word, and added her suggestions and corrected my mistakes. I had asked Linda to read my book as she was a former college English professor and a great editor. She loved my book, which gave me the encouragement to continue writing to the finish line.

I owe an apology to my computer. In my story, "Stop the World . . . ," I cast some aspersions upon my computer. Without your help, I could never have successfully finished my book. Your Internet has become a true friend, sharing so much information, and saving me hours of research at the library. Thank you computer; thank you Internet.

Part One
THE EARLY YEARS

FAMILY . . . a word that has been defined by so many. Our bloodline, our ancestry, our forebears, kinfolk, our relatives . . . the list goes on. George Santayana said, "Family is one of nature's masterpieces." Carson McCullers calls it, "The we of me." "The nucleus of civilization," writes Will Durant. And Pope John XXIII states, "The first and essential cell of human society." Family is the backbone of our existence.

AN INTRODUCTION TO MY HISTORY: MEET MY FAMILY

BOTH MY PARENTS, having been born of Russian immigrants, were raised with many siblings. My grandparents arrived in this country in the 1870s and 1880s, from Odessa, Kiev and Wilna.

Grandpa Meyer, my father's father, was born in 1861 in Wilna, Russia. He was a bantamweight pugilist when he arrived in this country. He was a successful fighter, until one day, he knocked out an opponent who never got up again. My grandfather feared he would be sent back to Russia, so in 1884 he joined the U.S. Army in the Wyoming Territory, serving for five years in the hospital corps. He was stationed at Fort Laramie, Wyoming. In later years, Grandpa Meyer became a successful builder of apartment houses in Brooklyn. He retired at the age of forty-five to a gentleman's farm in Monticello, New York.

My father's mother, Anna, had five children—four boys and a girl. We called her the "peanut grandma" because we frequently visited her on Sundays in Brooklyn, and she always gave us bags of raw peanuts. The shells landed all over the car going home. My father wasn't too happy.

My father, William, was very young when his family moved to Monticello. He grew up riding bareback on his horse. He was schooled, along with his siblings, in a one-room schoolhouse. Life was good. In 1917, my father attended Pratt Institute in Brooklyn, studying engineering, till 1919, when the family moved back to Brooklyn. His father lost most of his money and had to sell the farm. My father went to work to help the family, and in 1922 managed a men's store in War, West Virginia. In 1928, my dad entered Wall Street and worked as a "customer's man" in margin control, until 1932 at a firm that went under after the crash of Wall Street. Dad met and married my mother in 1930, and in 1932, moved to Hicksville, Long Island, and opened a hardware store.

My father and I were very close. When I was about ten years old, I vividly remember the two-mile walk home from Dad's store on a cold, snowy night while my father held my hand.

Celia, my mother's mother, born in 1871, gave birth to ten children. The tenth baby died at three months old, leaving my mother, the ninth child, as the youngest. I remember bringing Grandma purple grapes from the small vines we grew behind our house. She placed them in the bathtub and stomped on them barefoot, and made jugs of homemade wine. Mom let us sip the wine on special holidays.

My mother's father, Grandpa Henry, was born in Kiev in 1867, one of six children. He manufactured and owned retail stores of men's clothing in Brooklyn with his brother Joe, and also owned real estate. Grandpa spoke many languages which created a wonderful relationship with the many immigrants living in Brooklyn at the time. I believe it helped create the success he enjoyed.

My mother's family had many professionals . . . a few of some renown. Uncle Willie, my grandfather Henry's brother, was one of the doctors in the early 1900s, treating patients from the Henry Street Settlement . . . probably for free. The Henry Street Settlement was established in 1893 by Lillian Wald, and is still in existence today. Uncle Willie was very active in public health. The Museum of Natural History in New York has a series of lantern slides showing a doctor treating immigrants on the Lower East Side. The doctor is Uncle Willie. His sister, Aunt Kitty, married Leopold Cohen, an artist. They lived in England and he painted for royalty in Europe. Grandpa Henry's brother, Uncle Louie, owned a men's department store. He loved riding his horse in Central Park, almost to the end of his life. He died at the age of ninety-seven.

I adored my grandpa. Having nine children, he was blessed with many grandchildren. I was the first girl born eighteen years after the last granddaughter and he made me feel very special. He loved little girls; I knew I was his favorite. I was devastated when he died at the age of seventy-one. I was six years old, and still think of him to this day.

I'm so amazed when I hear the stories of the nineteenth-century immigrants to this country. They spoke little English, but they came to this country to seek greater opportunities. They came by steerage, on crowded ships, that were very uncomfortable and in rough seas. They hoped for a happier way of life and to be a free people. Nothing was going to stop them. They would work twenty-four hours a day, seven days a week, if they knew that would give them a better life.

My mother, Hilda, had quite a different life. Growing up the baby of nine children in Brooklyn, my mother was schooled in a city classroom. When she was in her late teens, her teacher recommended to her parents that she should attend college. She was extremely bright with a very high IQ. Her father, instead, wanted my mother to be the bookkeeper for his business and kept her close to home. As one of her duties, each day, my mother would have lunch with my grandfather in his limousine, as his chauffeur drove them through the park. My grandfather had reached the pinnacle of his success when my mother reached her teens. He was a wonderful man and loved his six girls and three boys dearly, but I believe he made a big mistake in keeping my mother from going to college.

My brothers, Mike and George, and I enjoyed a carefree and loving childhood. We had twenty-three cousins whom we saw frequently. Because my parents were the only members of the family that lived in the country, when I was young, our home was filled with aunts, uncles and cousins on many Sundays. My mother baked and cooked all weekend for our "famous" family dinners. I still remember the delicious aromas coming from the kitchen. Mom's reputation as a chef was impeccable.

I begged Mom to write her story, but she never did. She could have written another *A Tree Grows in Brooklyn*. Her family history was replete with humorous and fascinating stories. I remember my mother's laughter as she related some of these tales as I was growing up. Fortunately, I never forgot them; the following are the ones I remember.

Grandma Celia often took some of her nine children, perhaps five or six, on the trolley car to visit Grandpa at his men's store. She had a system of counting heads, as sometimes she travelled with all the children.

On this particular day, she left the store late and headed home to prepare dinner. Shortly after, the store was closed for the evening. It was the custom in those years for the cop on the beat to check the local stores to ensure they were locked. Checking Grandpa's store, he saw and heard, through the glass door of the shop, a small girl crying. Familiar with most of the shopkeepers, he went to my grandparents' home to inform them of the situation.

Aunt Rose had fallen asleep on a pile of men's slacks and was inadvertently left behind. Grandma had forgotten to count that day.

Growing up, I remained very close to my Aunt Rose and her family when they moved to Long Island. She married a musician, Uncle Rudy, who became one of the four main cellists of the New York Philharmonic. I loved sitting on the floor next to my uncle as he practiced his cello in preparation for his upcoming concerts. Together, they lived an incredible life, and I loved listening to all the stories my uncle related. He was a brilliant and funny storyteller. He played before the kings and queens of Europe and travelled the world also playing for the Longines Symphonette, which played much of the background music for so many famous movies. I still remember the story of Marilyn Monroe when she arrived for a rehearsal on a Saturday morning for her role in *"Gentlemen Prefer Blondes."* She was so gorgeous that the orchestra had a difficult time concentrating on the music.

Aunt Claire was my mother's oldest sister and the first-born. Being the eldest, she had the responsibility of taking care of some of the younger siblings. Walking one of the babies in her carriage one day (Claire was probably no more than eleven or twelve), she found some basement steps leading from the sidewalk, and let the carriage slip down the steps and walked home. She had had it!! Fortunately, the baby was fine and still sleeping when Grandma came to retrieve the "abandoned" child.

Aunt Claire was the funniest, most interesting and fascinating character in the family. Years later, she married Uncle Bennie, a theatrical agent. He was the agent for Houdini and Henny Youngman, among his many famous entertainers. As a couple, they were close friends of George Burns and Gracie Allen.

Aunt Claire was a beautiful young woman and was a cover girl on a magazine. She married very young—in her mid to late teens. Three weeks after her marriage, she "dolled up," putting on her makeup and prettiest dress, preparing to go out. When her husband asked her where she was going, her answer was, "On a date . . . I had this date before we were married."

As a young working girl in New York City, I frequently slept over at Aunt Claire's apartment when I had a date. They lived a block from Carnegie Hall. I never stopped laughing when I stayed over. Aunt Claire was a "pistol."

Mother's brother, my Uncle George, was the oldest of the three boys, and big for his age. George walked into an army recruiting station during World War I to sign up. He was very patriotic. He declared his age as eighteen. When they questioned him, one of the recruiters decided to take him home and receive his parents' permission. They discovered he was only fifteen.

My mother's sister, Sophie, was the most beautiful of all the girls; she was my godmother. She married Victor Bonomo, owner of the Gold Medal Candy Corporation. They made Bonomo's Turkish Taffy. When I was a child in camp, they would send me a large box of Turkish Taffy, Cracker Jacks and more. I became the most popular kid in camp when that box arrived. Everyone wanted to be my friend. I taught the kids how to crack the bar of Turkish Taffy, and occasionally some also cracked a tooth.

Oh! Mom! I wish you had written that book. You were a brilliant writer and you had so many stories to share with our family and the friends who loved you. I remember so much of your philosophy and your sage advice. "You never feel the brunt of a situation when you're running, it's when you stop . . . it hits you," is one of your quotes that has often surfaced throughout my life.

When I look back upon my growing-up years, I thank God for the blessings of family. I truly had a great base on which to build my own life.

Mom and Dad . . . two of the most influential and endearing people of my life

"Man's best friend"—a cliché we have often heard. The love of a pet for its master is perhaps the most loyal, unconditional and intense form of love we may ever experience.

THE STORY OF BOOTS

I WAS EIGHT YEARS OLD that cold, rainy Monday morning. Mom had just cleared the breakfast dishes and told us, my brothers and me, to get ready for school.

"Put your boots on, it's nasty outside. I'm driving you to school this morning," Mom said. "I don't want you waiting for the bus."

I stepped into the side-door vestibule where our boots sat in a pile on the floor. Fishing through the pile, I found my high, black galoshes.

I quickly pulled on the first boot and then the second. I couldn't get my foot all the way into the second boot. Then I felt something move inside the boot. I screamed. "Mom! There's a rat in my boot!"

My mother grabbed the boot off my foot and turned it upside down. Out came a little, black ball of fur with four, tiny, white front legs. The puppy blinked his eyes in the light. He had been sleeping inside the boot, probably for hours.

My brothers and I were so excited at the sight of this adorable little creature. Mom told us she and Dad had brought the puppy home late last night. It was one of a litter that my grandmother's dog had delivered that week. Mom had wanted to surprise us after we returned home from school on Monday. She knew we would be late getting to school if we knew about the puppy beforehand. And she was right.

I couldn't wait to get home from school. I thought about that adorable, little fluff of fur all day.

When the family gathered together that evening, we had the perfect name for the newest member of our family. *Boots* was so appropriate. Not only was he found inside my boot, but he had four, tiny white paws that made it look like he was wearing boots.

Boots grew up to be a lovable, protective dog, even though he wasn't very big. He followed us everywhere we went.

When I was nine years old, we moved to the other side of town. My father's store was in the center of town, about two miles from home. Each day, Boots took a long walk and visited my father at work. We never worried about him; he was always home, sitting in the driveway, to greet us when we returned from school. He was the best timekeeper I ever knew.

Boots' worst habit was chasing cars. We scolded him severely. But it didn't help. He loved the exciting and dangerous game. If he were human, he would probably have been a racecar driver.

When we arrived home from school one afternoon, we found Boots lying in the driveway, surrounded by our neighbors. His leg was broken in two places and he was very frightened.

Our neighbor had been riding his motorcycle past our house. Boots loved the thrill of this dangerous chase, but he was hit by the motorcycle. When Mom came home we took him to the veterinarian.

Boots remained in the veterinary hospital for a week. We hoped this terrible accident would quiet him down and he would give up his daring lifestyle.

He did settle down and become less active, especially when it came to chasing cars. But, it appeared he never forgot who hurt him so badly. He remembered our neighbor only <u>too</u> well.

One day, when our neighbor was walking past our house, Boots attacked him and ripped his pants. When my father came home that evening, he said Boots had to go.

The family was devastated. We had no choice. To keep Boots tied up would have broken his spirit. He was a "free soul" and loved roaming our small town.

My dad gave Boots to a farmer, who was a customer of my father's store. The farmer took him away in a truck, at night, so he would not be able to find his way home. The farmer lived many miles from us, but often visited my father with tales of Boots playing with his cats on the farm. *Boots had always hated cats*! My aunt said, "If Boots marries a cat, she'll have 'dittens' instead of kittens."

About a year later, the farmer told my father that Boots had run away. I remember how I cried.

Early one cold, November morning, my aunt was visiting for the weekend. She was sitting in the living room at the front of the house. She heard terrible scratching sounds on the front door. Peeking out the window, she saw a mongrel scratching on the storm door. Frightened, she ran to get my mother. Mom slowly opened the front door, protected behind the storm door, a second door that had been put up that week because of the cold weather.

Whimpering on our front steps was a bedraggled animal with burrs stuck all over its matted fur. One burr even caught the corner of his eye . . . another was stuck in his ear.

My mother opened the door and knelt down as Boots limped into my mother's arms.

She lifted Boots onto the kitchen counter and, one by one, removed the burrs from his fur, his eye, his ear and in between his paws. As my mother tried gently to pull out all the burrs, he kept licking my mother's hands.

Then came a warm bath. Boots never enjoyed being bathed, but this time he seemed to appreciate all the TLC he was receiving. As I towel-dried Boots and held him close, Mom prepared a feast of the ground beef we were having for dinner. Our meat loaf dinner became scrambled eggs.

A few years earlier, I had seen the movie, "*Lassie Come Home,*" and now I couldn't help comparing Boots' adventure with Lassie's. Boots had been running for many weeks. I don't know how he survived.

We were so happy to have Boots back home; we couldn't give him enough love. But soon, his old ways came back to haunt us. When he saw our neighbor he began chasing him again. He never forgot the pain.

Boots remained with us for another year, until the situation became too difficult to keep him.

My father finally informed the family that we were taking Boots to the Bideawee Home, an animal shelter on Long Island. Since 1903, this wonderful shelter kept dogs and cats until they could be adopted.

I was fifteen years old when I said my final goodbyes to one of my best friends . . . the dog I loved so dearly.

One cannot live on memories alone. One must seek to make each day memorable. Paste your memories in your mental scrapbook of life, and review those that warmed your heart . . . often. It helps to make new memories more meaningful.

TECHNICOLOR MEMORIES

I WAS NINE YEARS OLD when we moved into the house on Sixth Street. After years of renting in the little town of Hicksville, Long Island, a suburb of New York City, we finally owned our own home.

The house, in its simplicity, assumed the character of a child's drawing: a box-like square with a triangular roof, and a central door surrounded by double windows, like giant eyes blinking their welcome through half-open shades. In contrast, the grounds were quite magnificent.

Bright yellow and tangerine marigolds ran along the short front walk, complimenting the brown weather-beaten shingles. The woman who had owned the house loved flowers, and left us a legacy of breath-taking beauty—which began in the early spring and faded in the late fall.

Majestic purple irises, snuggled between red and white azalea bushes, lined one side of the driveway. Opposite, was the side of the house that held my room. Morning glories, the color of a deep-blue summer sky, climbed the vines clinging to the shingles, reaching toward my window. Each morning, they awoke—their bright, soft petals forming a small trumpet. By late afternoon, their petals began to close, preparing for a long night's sleep. They were my favorite.

My mother loved the magnificent array of lavender lilac trees, which bordered the garage, at the rear of the house. In spring, she filled the house with the tall-stemmed, puffy blossoms, emitting their sweet, perfumed fragrance.

On a long stretch of lawn which continued from the backyard, fruit trees blossomed. Peach, plum and sickle pear stood in line like tree soldiers carrying their bounty. They filled our kitchen with delicious aromas. Mom made great peach pie! In summer, croquet balls clicked and clattered through their hoops on the open expanse.

During World War II, we planted a victory garden behind the garage. Tomatoes, zucchini, string beans, carrots . . . the profuse abundance of vegetables kept my mother and me busy canning and storing wonderful edibles for the winter. The glass jars lined the pantry shelves, displaying their crayon colors—oranges, purples, greens, reds.

Huge maple trees bordered the street in front of the house. An artist's palette of colors trickled off the trees by a gentle breeze in early fall. The crimsons, golds and purples were swept into mounds of crisp, dry leaves. After days of leaf jumping, with my brothers, from one crunchy mound to another, the leaves were reswept and burned, filling the air with their pungent odor.

Bushy-tailed squirrels raced frantically from tree to tree, hoarding their acorns for the coming winter, only stopping to take a quick nibble.

Winter was a wonderland of marshmallow evergreens and slender locust trees, their outstretched branches laden with silvery icicles, creaking in the cold wind. Tiny chickadees tweeted their little tunes, reminding one that spring would soon return.

Time has neither dimmed nor daunted my memory of Mother Nature's magnificent seasons. The grounds and gardens of my home still remain in brilliant Technicolor.

From the minds of children are sometimes borne the greatest adventures.

THE WEEPING WILLOW TREE

THE GREAT ATLANTIC HURRICANE in September, 1944, pounded Long Island, New York, with a ferocity my family had rarely encountered. New York City sustained hurricane force winds of 81 mph, with gusts up to 99 mph. The worst of the storm hit the eastern end of Long Island, as a category three hurricane, but, even though my home was in mid-island, the effects of the storm were still devastating. The hurricane caused $1,000,000 in damages on the eastern half of Long Island alone.

My father took the family into the basement of our house. We had no protection for our windows, which, fortunately, were average sized double-hung windows. Our home had no large "picture windows."

When the worst of the storm had subsided, we crept back upstairs and went to bed. But the storm continued through the night.

My brothers shared a bedroom at the back of the house. My younger brother's bed was under the window next to the back of the house.

When the calm arrived the following morning, we discovered the seventy-foot Weeping Willow tree had fallen into the backyard. The tree had stood less than twenty feet from the back wall of the house. Some of the branches would sweep our roof on windy days. Had the tree fallen in the opposite direction, against the house, my brother could have been seriously injured.

We went outside to assess the damage. My parents were very unhappy at having lost our beautiful, old tree, which served as a giant umbrella, shielding us from the intense summer sun. We often enjoyed picnics under the protection of this towering specimen. Although my parents were thankful no one was injured, they were downhearted at the loss of our majestic tree.

My brothers and I wandered inside the fallen tree. It was, perhaps, forty-five feet tall on its side. The interior of the tree was very light and open, as the graceful branches left room for the sunlight it had always enjoyed. We were fascinated. It was another world, and so beautiful walking among the pliant branches. We were very excited and decided we knew what we wanted to do. We stepped out into the sunlight with smiles on our faces. Our parents weren't smiling . . . but we were.

We gathered all our neighborhood friends for a big pow-wow, and told them to meet at our house that following day. We announced our plan to take advantage of the fallen tree. Everyone was excited. Our backyard was now named, "the jungle."

Every day, after school that September, the children gathered at our house. My brother, Mike, assumed the role of Tarzan. I became, Jane, and my younger brother, George, was Boy. My dog, Boots, even had a role, and became Cheetah. Our friends were the natives. Some were the "good guys" and others were the enemy. They took turns.

Mike swung from pliant branch to branch inside the tree, howling Tarzan's famous call of the jungle. We hunted for food, which we hid in strategic places, especially bananas. We fought the bad natives, and always won.

The fun and excitement of our game went on for weeks. Even friends who didn't live in our neighborhood begged to be a part of it. Word of our exciting adventure got around and everyone wanted to see the famous tree.

My father hired a man to cut the tree into firewood. Dad told us we could enjoy our game as long as the tree still existed. It took about six weeks before there wasn't enough left of the tree to continue our fantasy.

But, even though we all missed the towering magnificence of our Weeping Willow tree, the tree, in its final farewell, left my brothers and me a beautiful gift. The memory of our "jungle" adventure remains with me till this day.

A smile, given away, is another coin dropped into the "piggy bank" of your heart.

A GRATEFUL SMILE

IN THE SUMMER OF 1953, in New York City, I was walking on Fifth Avenue, strolling back to work. I noticed a man in uniform walking towards me. He was slender, well-built and of medium height. As he neared, he removed his hat; it was a very warm day.

When he came closer, I looked up, and to my horror saw his face had been obliterated. He was a man without a face.

I tried to avert my eyes, but he slowed and looked directly at me. I looked back and smiled. The biggest smile I could muster.

Shortly after he passed me, I realized I was in front of Lord & Taylor. I needed to stop at the cosmetic counter, so I went into the store. Moments later, I felt a tap on my shoulder. I turned to face the man without a face.

"Thank you for that beautiful smile; you made my day." And then he walked away.

The lady behind the cosmetic counter looked at me in astonishment, but didn't say anything. I walked back to work thinking about this man, who had, most likely, been a casualty of the Korean War. He had a beautiful, soft voice. I imagined he had been a good-looking young man before this horrid tragedy befell him.

But, my heart was full, knowing that he enjoyed the pleasure of a smile from a young girl.

Recently, I was waiting at the curb about to cross a street in Manhattan. A young woman was standing next to me. I noticed a distressed look on her face, as if she were about to cry. When she turned to look at me, I offered a warm smile. Then I asked, "Are you alright?"

She hesitated, then said, "I'm fine. Your smile helped," then walked away in the opposite direction.

I love to smile at babies and young children; their responses delight me.

I find myself humming the tune "Smile" while walking on the streets of Manhattan. Growing up, my dad loved listening to Nat King Cole, who originally sang "Smile," which charted in 1954.[1]

Michael Jackson sang it; it was his favorite song, according to Brooke Shields. His brother, Jermaine, sang "Smile" at his memorial service in July, 2009.[2]

"Smile" has been recorded by: Natalie Cole, Diana Ross, Chick Corea, Josh Groban, Perry Como, Luis Miguel, Michael Bolton, Judy Garland, Barbra Streisand and Tony Bennett . . . the list goes on.[3]

When I researched the song, I discovered it was composed by Charlie Chaplin as an instrumental theme in the soundtrack for his 1936 movie, *Modern Times*. In 1954, the lyrics were added by John Turner and Geoffrey Parsons.[4]

My favorite line is the last:

> *You'll find that life is still worthwhile,*
> *If you just smile.*

My "piggy bank" has been overflowing for years.

Never think you are better than anyone. You are a better person when you think others are as good as you. But, to love oneself is not selfish—it is selfless.

IF YOU'VE GOT IT . . . FLAUNT IT

ON A SATURDAY NIGHT, when I was twenty-one, I dressed in my sexiest dress, for a date with my soon-to-be fiancé. I wore a dress my designer had given me, which had been fitted to my body. I was a fashion model, pre-college, during college and post-college years. The dress was a red and white flowered cotton, sprinkled with red sequins.

I floated down the steps of my house, feeling like a princess. My parents waited at the foot of the stairs with proud smiles on their faces.

As I reached the bottom step, my father reached up to close the open neckline.

"Da—dee," I exclaimed. "It's a surplus neckline." In fashion lingo that's a bodice with fabric crisscrossed over the bust-line.

"I know it's surplus, but you don't have to show it all," my dad said, snidely.

My mother then stepped in front of my father, opened the neckline back to its original position, and stated, "If you've got it . . . flaunt it."

That summer, I was runner-up in a beauty contest held at the beach club I belonged to, in Long Beach, New York. Was my surplus neckline an influence?

My parents were into developing good self-esteem in their children, but, no big egos with swelled heads were allowed in my home.

My two brothers excelled at almost everything they attempted, but, they were two of the most fun-loving, non-egotistical guys I ever knew. My older brother, Myles, (Mike for short) became an obstetrician/gynecologist at Kaiser Permanente in California. He also had a magnificent bass-baritone voice and studied opera. Sadly, I lost my brother, Mike, three and a half years ago; he had been afflicted with Parkinson's disease for twenty years. My younger brother, George, became a mechanical engineer, and eventually built his own business, designing and manufacturing locks and door hardware. George was also talented musically, and played the trumpet. He played with his own group as a teenager, and then, in his freshman year in college, joined the union and played professionally with a local band, until my mother put an end to that.

I believe my brothers achieved their success in life without enormous egos, because of the way we were raised.

The lessons I learned from my family kept me on a steady course throughout my life.

I have always been "comfortable in my own skin," but never considered that I was better than anyone else.

Self-esteem is at the top of the list of the gifts we can bestow upon our children.

I believe when one can love oneself, one can love the world. I also believe everyone is born with something special to offer this world. That "something" needs to be nourished, so it can grow.

Feel good about yourself because we're all special.

Be impressed—not by what one is on the outside, but, what one is on the inside.

IMPRESSIONS

GROWING UP IN THE small town of Hicksville, Long Island, New York, taught me many lessons about life. In later years, living the city life in Manhattan, and travelling the world, I felt a balance and perspective that I may not have achieved, had I not experienced life in the "boondocks" compared to life in the "big city."

My parents moved to Hicksville in 1932, during the Depression. Recently married, my mother left behind a wealthy family to marry my father, who had lost everything, for love. Dad had an opportunity to buy a hardware store (it was something he knew a little about) in Hicksville. Mom worked, side-by-side with my dad, whenever she could, while juggling raising three children.

My mother was gifted in so many ways. She was a woman with a brilliant mind and a high IQ. In later years, working as a bookkeeper for a detective agency, she was asked to run the agency. She had a knack of always finding a way out of the proverbial "box" to resolve almost any situation.

Her warmth and outgoing nature drew people to her. In our small town, there weren't many women like my mother. She had many friends quite different from herself. She saw the good in people and was accepting of most. Having grown up the youngest of nine children, she was able to address the differences in people, as she did with her own family.

Mom's talent for writing was exceptional. Her letters throughout my life, especially when I was in college, were like essays. Had my professor graded them . . . they would have received A-pluses.

What truly made my mother outstanding, was not only the loving, selfless devotion to her family and friends, it was her wisdom. She would often say, "You can find the good in people if you choose to look deep enough." My mother remained my best friend throughout my life.

Mom realized, when I was becoming a young woman, I needed more of an expanded social life than was offered living in a small town. When I was sixteen, Mom sent me to modeling school on the L.I. Railroad, every Saturday morning for almost a year.

When I was seventeen, after graduating from high school, I went to Syracuse University. I wanted to be a fashion designer and enrolled in the School of Fine Arts. During the summer I worked as a model in Manhattan.

Again, my mother wanted to expose me to a more socially interesting and fulfilling lifestyle, than was offered to a young girl commuting to work from the suburbs.

When I was nineteen and twenty years old, my mom suggested that I go to the country on weekends and holidays, whenever I was able to get away. The Concord Hotel in the Catskills was the hotel of choice, as it wasn't too far from New York City, and my cousin, Tico, who worked with his father, had a great relationship with the management. His company, the Gold Medal Candy Corporation, held their conventions there. My cousin introduced me to the management, and from then on, I was treated like family. I was invited to many of the private parties held for the stars and entertainers. I met and became friendly with some of the singers, comedians and entertainers of that era. One of my most memorable evenings was chatting with Billy Eckstein, the singer, during a private party celebrating his engagement. I loved his voice, but I was more impressed with the gentleman that he was.

I could list so many names from television and Hollywood that I enjoyed spending time with, but I won't. It's not important. What is important is that I realized, at a young age, to look for the person under the veneer of success. Some of those I met I would have loved to keep as good friends. Others? Absolutely not!

In the summer of my twenty-first year, late one afternoon, I was sunning myself at a beach club. Trying to achieve a tan, while holding a sun-visor under my face, with my eyes closed, I heard a voice.

"If you want to get a tan, why don't you come down to the beach earlier?"

Who was this brash, annoying person?

I looked up and saw a very handsome young man. I thought, "*What nerve!*" I continued sunning myself. With eyes closed, I ignored him.

Moments later, he sat down next to me on the chaise lounge. He began chatting away, till I finally had to put down the visor.

"I see you enjoy doing the *Times* crossword puzzle. I do, too. How about doing it together?" I gave up the idea of getting a fresh tan and tried to be polite. I was dating someone fourteen years older than myself who had been divorced. He treated me like a princess. I wasn't interested in a "kid."

"My name is David. What's yours?"

We talked for about a half hour and he told me he had been medically discharged from the army; it was after the Korean War. He was twenty-two years old. Then he asked, "What are you doing tomorrow night?"

"I'm busy."

"What are you doing the next night?"

I replied, "I'm busy the next eight nights, except for Thursday; I promised my mother I would stay home and spend the evening with her."

"Call your mother."

"No . . . I can't do that."

"Call your mother," he insisted.

I called my mother. We went out that Thursday night. Two weeks later, he asked me to marry him. I told him he was *crazy*. We didn't know each other. He said that was okay, and he would ask me every two weeks till I said yes. And he did.

At the age of twenty-two, David was more confident and self-assured than any man I had known; he was mature beyond his years. He knew what he wanted and he went after it till he got it. And he wanted me. That was very appealing. He was a very passionate person and was also very good-looking. When I brought him home to meet my parents, they saw everything I saw in him. My mom said, "He could sell you the Brooklyn Bridge twice, and you wouldn't even realize it."

David grew up in a Bronx apartment sharing a room with his sister. His dad was a partner in a women's garment company. His mom went to work when he was eight years old to help with the family's finances. David learned great work ethics at a very young age, which he kept throughout his life. He knew he was going to be successful and was determined to have his own garment company one day. He had so much ambition; nothing was going to stop him. He graduated high school at sixteen, and graduated college at twenty. Drafted after college during the Korean War, his first job, after he was discharged, was as an assistant buyer for Robert Hall, the major retailer. David was honest and sincere . . . almost to a fault. He often repeated his father's quote, "You do what's right, let the other person do the wrong thing." He had a great sense of humor and loved telling a good joke. His voice was strong and compelling; when David spoke, you listened. I saw everything in him that I wanted for my future. David won me over; the chemistry was too powerful to resist. My mind and my heart said "*go for it.*"

Why did he want to marry me after knowing me for such a short time? Only David could answer that.

At twenty-one years old, having dated extensively, I thought I might spend my life as an old maid.

Where was true love, and how would I know it if I found it? Eros, the God of Love, had other plans for me. When his arrow pierced my heart, I knew I had found it.

My Wedding Toast

Almost six months to the day we met, I was engaged, and four months later we were married.

My mother was right. I saw what was inside . . . and I was very IMPRESSED.

1955, married three months

Watch and listen carefully to young children. You may see and hear hints of who they may become.

TINA: A LIFE'S JOURNEY THROUGH MUSIC

WHEN MY DAUGHTER, Tina, was a three-year-old, I would hear singing from her room early in the morning. That was the signal that she had awakened to greet the day.

She romped around the house, often humming and singing little tunes.

When she turned four, allergies took hold of her young digestive system, and she began having painful tummy-aches. She would lie on her stomach across an ottoman to help relieve the discomfort. She no longer awoke singing her morning repertoire.

After extensive tests, it was discovered that she had an allergy to wheat and gluten. Her doctor suggested I feed her hot oatmeal for breakfast, as it would soothe her stomach and she could tolerate the oats.

The first try offered me a big "YUK," and she refused to eat it. I asked the doctor, "How do I get her to eat hot oatmeal?"

"Tell her a story. You're good at that," he answered. And so I did. It worked!

I wrote a story about a singing princess named Tina, who had a tummy-ache. When Tina ate her "special" hot oatmeal each morning, she always asked to hear her story. Little did I know then, that music and singing would become an integral part of her life. From the "singing princess" to today, Tina's life has been flowing on a river of music.

Throughout Tina's school years, she was always involved with choir or chorus. In elementary school, she sang with her second grade chorus in a professional recording studio for a compilation album that had performances from every grade, kindergarten through high school.

When Tina was thirteen years old, she wrote a song for a book report at school, and sang it the next day in front of her class. The class was quite surprised by Tina's creativity and talent, and rewarded her with generous applause.

At the age of fifteen, Tina attended a performing arts summer camp. She learned some basic guitar skills, so she could accompany herself as she sang for the "Coffee House" talent show. The song was "Longer," by Dan Fogelberg. She practiced the chords for weeks on end, so much so, that her bunkmates forced her outside the bunk to practice. The song was incessantly playing in their heads, even when she was not singing it. The night came, and Tina was called up to the stage. Clutching the guitar, with butterflies in her stomach, she started her accompaniment, and sang in a beautiful, angelic voice. In the middle of the song, she froze, as she could not remember the next chord. The crowd was so silent you could hear a pin drop. After taking a deep breath to center herself, the memory came back, and she continued to play and sing.

The lovely melody continued and then . . . she froze again! She could have walked off the stage in a panic, but instead, she again focused, taking in a long, deep breath, as the silent crowd tingled with anticipation. Tina knew that everyone in the audience was pulling for her; she was fully engaged in her commitment to follow through and finish the song.

She continued to the end. When the song was over, the crowd roared and screamed with delight and adoration. She did it!! She faced the challenge, the fear, and mistakes, and lived to tell about it! For the rest of that summer at camp, she became somewhat of a rock star. People she didn't even know would approach her with congratulations and praise for her courage, perseverance, and wonderful performance. Tina learned a great lesson that summer. Never give up on something you know you can do well. The guitar wasn't one of her fortes, but her singing definitely was.

We encouraged her singing and the following year she was given private lessons from a prominent vocal coach. When we attended a recital the coach had arranged, her father and I were "blown away" by her voice and stage presence.

In high school, she travelled to different cities and countries, including England, where she sang inside Westminster Abbey, with her high school chorale.

She auditioned, and was chosen for All-County Choir in her senior year of high school.

Again, she joined the chorus when she went to college, and studied vocal performance as a double major, along with psychology, at Syracuse University.

After graduating college, she spent a short time working for her father and then enrolled at New York University for a master's program in music therapy. Though she did not choose a career in music therapy, Tina gained a great understanding of clinical interactions and the power of music as a healing tool.

In 2004, Dr. Tina Pearl graduated from chiropractic college (Palmer

West), and integrated her knowledge and passion for music with the tools and techniques she learned in chiropractic school, to create *Chiromusic*. Chiromusic is a groundbreaking approach to help the body, mind and spirit on its journey of healing. Tina uses a variety of bodywork techniques, including chiropractic manipulation, massage and soft tissue techniques, along with soothing and transformative music. She uses guided visualizations and imagery to help her patients shift into a world of relaxation and release.

Tina wrote, sang, and recorded a beautiful ballad for her friend's wedding. The song, "Love is a Gift," was presented as a lasting gift of the occasion. Earlier, Tina had written and sung a song for her father's sixty-fifth surprise birthday party. Four years later, when her father passed away at the age of sixty-nine, she sang the song again, at his funeral.

Tina continues to frequent Karaoke clubs to exercise her love of music and singing.

Clearly, the little "princess" is still inside my daughter. Tina often reminds me of her "special" story, and we both enjoy the memory, over a bowl of hot oatmeal.

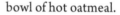

See the story of "Princess Tina's Tummy-ache" in the Appendix

1969—"Princess Tina"— three years old with her brothers Cliff, twelve, and Todd, nine

Our children often live what they learn. Hopefully, they adopt our better traits and the lessons we impose upon them. Compassion is a big one.

AT THE AGE OF FOURTEEN, my son, Cliff was a newspaper delivery boy.

One snowy, very cold February night, I arrived home with his younger brother and sister from a doctor's appointment. Cliff answered the door with a big, impish smile on his face; I knew something had happened.

He was delivering his papers, when he realized he was being followed by a dog. It was a Sheltie—a small version of a Collie.

When he returned home, the Sheltie was beside him. Upon examination, he discovered the dog had a collar, but no tags. He didn't have the heart to turn him away, so he kept him in our basement till I returned home.

He begged us to keep him, but, we already had a dog . . . a short-haired Schnauzer. Because of the children's allergies, it was many years before the doctor allowed us to have a dog, and we simply couldn't keep two, especially not a long-haired dog.

Cliff made me promise to help him find the owner, and not to call the dog pound to take him away. I promised. We proceeded to try to find the owner, in various ways, all to no avail.

We took the dog for a check-up to our veterinarian, as I was concerned that the dog might be diseased and pass something on to our dog or even to the children.

Finally, after nine days, we brought the dog to the North Shore Animal League—a place that kept animals for adoption. The Sheltie was soon adopted by a wonderful family.

The story of Cliff had to be told. This true tale happened a long time ago, but the compassion and the feelings of a fourteen-year-old remain as fresh today. Cliff became a lawyer and moved to Denver, Colorado, and after a few years was elected Chairman of the Board for the Colorado SIDS Program. When I asked him what made him take on the position, since he had no close friends that lost a child from SIDS, this is what he answered. "I wanted to help provide a resource and support for families who had lost babies from SIDS." Cliff is one of the most altruistic persons I have ever known. The following is the children's story I wrote in honor of my son.

CLIFF'S TEETH CHATTERED as he pulled off his gloves and blew hot breath into his cupped hands. "It's getting dark and it's starting to snow again, fella. I've delivered my last paper and I'm goin' home. You'd better head home too."

The dog nuzzled Cliff's hand, begging for another caress. "You've followed me for an hour. It's chow time! I'm starved and I'm cold, and you must be too. GO HOME BOY! GO HOME!"

Cliff picked up his bike and walked it through the crusted snow onto the ice-covered road, while the wind sent shivers through his jeans. The dog followed.

"Look here, fella," said Cliff, speaking gently to the panting animal. "I don't know who you belong to—you have no tags—but, I can't keep you." The dog barked excitedly, sending puffs of steam into the frigid air.

"Okay! You win!"

When Cliff arrived home he noticed the car was missing from the garage. He slowly opened the door to the house, waiting for the usual, excited yapping of Misty, the family's Schnauzer. "Down Misty! Quiet! Mom! Is anybody home?" There was no answer.

Misty greeted the new dog and sniffed her, but the dog seemed scared and clung to Cliff. "Come on boy—into the basement with you."

"Hi honey! We're home!" yelled Cliff's mother, minutes later. "I took the kids for their allergy shots and we got stuck at the doctor's office."

"Mom . . . I have something to show you," said Cliff, reluctantly.

"Cliff, can it wait? I'm late getting dinner."

"Please Mom! Now!"

"What is it? What is it?" demanded five-year-old Tina.

"It's the Cookie Monster," mocked Cliff's younger brother, Todd, as they all marched down to the basement.

"Wow!" yelled Todd.

Mom grabbed Tina as she lunged for the dog. "No Tina! Don't touch him! Cliff! You're fourteen years old. When are you going to stop bringing home every stray animal you find?" Mom was really upset.

"Please . . . listen Mom. I couldn't leave him to starve and freeze in this cold. He has no tags and . . ." Cliff continued to tell his story.

"Oo—kay! We'll discuss it with Dad. But . . . in the meantime, he must remain in the basement, and no one is to come down here to play with him. Cliff, you can only come down to feed him."

That evening, Dad listened to Cliff's woeful tale.

"You're a Good Samaritan, Cliff, but with the allergies in this family, two dogs are too much. What do you want to do?"

"I know we can't keep him Dad, but, we can try to find his owner. Someone must be pretty unhappy about his missing dog. Tomorrow, I'll ask the principal to make an announcement."

"I'll do the same in my school!" Todd added enthusiastically.

"Me too!" shouted Tina.

That night, Cliff went to the basement to bring the dog some water. *He's so beautiful,* he thought. *He looks just like Lassie.*

When the children came home from school the following day, no one had good news.

"Hi, boy! Did you miss me?" The dog raced back and forth, barking a big hello. He jumped up, almost knocking Cliff over, and tried to lick his face. "Down, boy! I know you're lonely. I'm sorry, but Mom thinks you might be diseased. Eat your dinner; I'll be back later. Be a good boy."

Cliff called the local radio station about the lost dog. He notified other local schools and placed advertisements in two newspapers; it was futile.

After two days, Cliff's mother decided to take the dog to the veterinarian, since "Boy," as everyone called him, remained an uninvited guest.

"Handsome dog," said Dr. Goodman. "He's not a Collie though, Cliff, he's a Sheltie; that's a pretty fine breed. They make good guard dogs. Look at his snout; he has a scar across it—probably from pushing his nose through a chain-link fence."

Cliff asked many questions while Dr. Goodman continued to examine Boy.

"Yes, Cliff. He's in good health, but, I'm going to give him some shots. He's about five years old. He's been running for quite some time. Look at the pads of his feet; they're swollen and bruised."

"Do you think we have a chance of finding his owner?" asked Cliff.

"I doubt it. It looks to me like someone removed his tags and set him loose, a good distance from here, so he couldn't find his way home."

Cliff's heart sank. He barely heard Dr. Goodman tell his mother he couldn't accept her money. "Anyone kind enough to take home a lost dog deserves my services free," said Dr. Goodman, smiling at Cliff. "Have you ever heard of a place called the Animal League? It shelters animals until they can find a home for them."

"Great!" yelled Cliff, his heart pounding with new hope. "I'll call tomorrow."

Cliff made arrangements to bring Boy for an "interview" on Saturday morning. The woman at the animal shelter was very kind. "Right now, we don't have room to take Boy. We only have facilities for twenty-three dogs. You'll have to wait until we get an opening."

Cliff was crushed.

"He seems so attached to you," said the woman.

"Yeah . . . I know," muttered Cliff.

"Don't worry. Be patient."

Cliff walked away—a lump swelling in his throat. "I promise you Boy, I'll never abandon you, or let the dog pound get their mitts on you. I promise!"

The week dragged by, made all the worse by the thought of having to eventually give Boy away. On Friday, Cliff arrived home from school as the phone rang.

"May I speak to Cliff Pearl? This is the Animal League calling."

"Speaking. . . ."

"Cliff, you may bring Boy tomorrow. We had a couple in here yesterday that is looking for a dog for their ranch. They have five children and seemed most interested when I told them about Boy."

Cliff could barely say "thanks," as he hung up the phone.

On Saturday, the entire Pearl family brought Boy to the Animal League.

"He's a beauty!" said Mr. Makko, the man who was interested in adopting Boy. "Thank you, Cliff. Thank you very much. We heard how you rescued this poor animal from certain death. He'll be very happy, as he'll have plenty of room to roam free, and he'll get a lot of lovin'."

Cliff shook hands with the gentleman and nodded his response—his heart both happy and sad. "Don't forget me Boy!" yelled Cliff, as he ran to the car ahead of his family—the tears flooding his eyes. The dog began to whimper, as if he knew he would never see Cliff again.

"Cliff . . . wait!" yelled his mother, as she ran to catch up with him. She put her arm around his shoulder. "It's good to cry—for both good and bad things. It puts everything in perspective," said his mother, jokingly, as she blew her nose. "It's alright, honey. No problem."

"I'm okay, Mom. I love Boy, but I realize that sometimes a part of loving is being able to let go, and it hurts. Besides, I'm not the one with the problem . . . you are."

"What problem?" asked his mother.

"Your mascara's running!"

Visit the lands of those who live a different culture, practice different traditions, and speak another language. Open your heart and mind to all. We have so much to learn from so many others.

IN 1965, MY HUSBAND and I took our first trip to California. We had been married ten years and, next to our honeymoon in the Virgin Islands, had travelled no further, by car, than a few hours from home.

In 1968, I had three children, and travelling abroad would have been difficult.

While visiting my parents, living in Florida, my mother overheard a conversation between my husband and me about travelling. What I heard next opened the way for a *wanderlust* that exists to this day.

"If you would like to take a trip, I would be happy to stay with the children," my mother said.

When we returned home we *raced* to get our passport photos and apply for our passports. We made plans for our first trip abroad the following year.

OUR WANDERLUST I: 1969-1975

1969: Our first trip abroad we headed to London for ten days. We tried to see every site possible within the time we were there. Buckingham Palace, Windsor Castle, the museums, shopping at Harrods, and of course, the London Theatre, were among the many attractions we enjoyed. When we finally arrived back in the USA, it took us about a week to rid ourselves of our English accents.

1969—A sunny day visiting Windsor Castle

1970: Rome. What an historical and exciting city. Visiting the Vatican was an adventure. We visited all the ancient sites of the city, including the Coliseum;

the Pantheon; the Roman Forum; and two great museums. We loved visiting Piazza Navona, where tartufo, the delicious ice-cream dessert, originated, and is still served in the cafes along the Piazza. For us, this was a big draw to this beautiful Piazza with its magnificent fountains, especially on warm evenings. We indulged.

Shopping was a fun pastime. I had been warned that on occasion an admiring Italian might pinch you on the rear. I was viewing some wonderful clothes in a store window when I felt a pinch on my rear. I turned around to admonish David. It wasn't David.

On a beautiful, sunny day we took the train to Florence. Walking across the Ponte Vecchio, a medieval bridge built across the Arno River, was a dazzling experience for a woman but not so wonderful for a man. Lining either side of the bridge are jewelry shops, one after the other. The bridge had a golden glow.

1970—Just returning from a spree on the Ponte Vecchio—A happy, smiling Mona! A happy, smiling David??

The sites of Rome were memorable, but I knew I would return someday. The people were warm and gracious, but the real reason . . . the food . . . mmmmm-yum.

November, 1972: We had moved to Florida in June of 1972. This was much easier for my mother's *expertise* in watching grandchildren, as my parents lived fifteen minutes away. Though I had a housekeeper I loved, Mom was still the "chief supervisor."

We were off to Paris on a cold November day. We had never been to Paris before. Although we enjoyed visiting all the wonders and important sites of this beautiful and romantic city; it was the magnificent food that made up for the frigid weather.

Paris, 1972—A day visit to Versailles . . . Brrrrrr

1975: Our twentieth wedding anniversary trip; it was the most adventurous trip we had ever undertaken.

We arrived back in Paris on our anniversary in June. It was unusually cool and rainy. After spending the day roaming around the city, walking between the raindrops, we headed to our hotel. We cancelled opera tickets for the evening, as the weather worsened and we were exhausted. We ordered dinner—in bed—and remained there for the evening. What a way to spend an anniversary!

Two days later, we flew to Cannes. The Côte d'Azur (French Riviera) is breathtaking. The areas and the countries surrounding the Mediterranean are some of the most picturesque in the world.

Cannes—1975 The Côte d'Azur

Our hotel was on the beach. I did something I had never done before, and would never do again. I went *topless*.

When we settled ourselves on the beach, my husband noticed that women of all ages were topless. He suggested I do the same.

"Not me," I answered.

But then he dared me. I am not one to take a dare lightly. I ripped off the top of my bikini, stood up, and took a long walk along the water. To my surprise . . . no one noticed. I felt so free . . . almost like a child again. But, I prayed I wouldn't meet anyone I knew.

While in Cannes, we hired a driver to take us on a tour of the Riviera. Arriving in Monte Carlo, David asked the driver to wait outside while we went into the famous casino. (*Picture James Bond at the tables.*) David, nonchalantly, stepped up to the roulette table, placed a large chip on number 6 (for the month of our anniversary), and the next thing we heard was the

croupier announcing, "*Nombre six.*" WE WON! We walked out, fifteen minutes after arriving, back to our driver and continued our day trip.

While in Monte Carlo, we drove up to the Palace in Monaco, hoping to catch a glimpse of Princess Grace.

In front of the Palace in Monaco

David (my king) relaxing at the Theatre of Dionysus

After a glorious visit to the Côte d'Azur, we continued on to Athens. One can be overwhelmed by the remaining edifices that tell the history of Greece. The Acropolis sits high on a rocky crag, 230 feet above the city of Athens. The remnants of the Acropolis include the Parthenon, still sitting proudly with its many friezes displaying its days of glory. One is taken back in time, when the gods of history dwelled here.

We stopped to rest in the Theatre of Dionysus, built in 534 B.C., where thirteen thousand citizens gathered on sixty-seven tiers during the Dionysian spring festivals.

We loved the food in Greece and spent a fun evening in a typical *taverna*. The music was lively and people were dancing. The waiter placed a pile of plates in the middle of our table. We asked what the plates were for and were told they were to throw on the floor.

My husband said, "NO WAY." Within fifteen minutes, when people were throwing the plates, while others were dancing, my husband picked up the plates and threw them onto the floor. Then we got up and joined the dancing

The following day we left Athens and boarded the ship, the *Stella Solaris*, to begin our visit to the Greek Islands and Egypt.

Mykonos, Santorini and Rhodes are stunningly beautiful islands, but Crete remained my favorite; I could see and touch the remains of the fascinating history of the Minoan civilization. The queen's bathtub, still intact, was fed by the water which ran from above through a series of halved clay pipes . . . early plumbing. I could visualize her, luxuriating in her bath, being attended by her servants.

We continued our journey aboard the ship to Egypt, arriving in the harbor of Alexandria. The trip into Cairo was memorable. First stop was the Cairo Museum, which housed the King Tut exhibit. Afterwards we went shopping.

We were told to bargain with the shopkeepers. Never accept the first price. We found some boxes with inlaid ivory that we loved. David asked the price. The bargaining went back and forth for about twenty minutes, till David said we had to leave, as the bus was outside waiting for us.

The shopkeeper threw up his arms and said, exasperated, "OKAY! Are you cheap?" We bought the boxes.

The streets of Cairo

Shopping in the market in Cairo

We also bought two *galabias* or *abayas* (traditional robes worn by men and women), and a *kaffiyeh* (the traditional headdress for men, a diagonally folded square of cloth held down with a cord around the head).

There was a costume ball aboard ship within a few days, and David thought we could dress as traditional Egyptians. We asked four beautiful, young women to be part of our harem. The night of the costume ball, we marched, six of us in a line, in the parade of costumes around the room. David was the sheik, his arms folded across his chest, and dressed in his *abaya*. I followed, dutifully behind, in my *galabia*, a veil across my face, as number one wife. Behind me followed the four beauties dressed in harem garb. The judges were overwhelmed. WE WON!

Sheik David and his number one wife

Visiting the Pyramids and the Sphinx was an experience. I had assumed they were somewhere in the middle of the desert, but, to my amazement, they are located close to the edge of the city of Cairo.

We rode camels across the open areas and I went down into the catacombs, even though I have claustrophobia. It was dark and musty.

The last leg of our trip took us to Spain, and the capital city of Madrid. Located in the center of the Iberian Peninsula, with its high altitude, Madrid's climate is warm and dry in the summer and cool in the winter.

There was so much to see and not enough time to see it all, but we managed to enjoy many of Madrid's wonderful offerings, including the Prado Museum and Pablo Picasso's famous masterpiece *Guernica* at the Museo Reina Sofía.

Someday I would love to return to this beautiful city with its hospitable people and its great paella.

After a day trip to Toledo, we continued on to Seville, a city known for its famous bullfights. We were exited to experience this great event, but we did not really enjoy it. The crowds cheered and screamed, "Olé!" But we felt it was a very cruel sport, reminding us of the gladiators who fought to their deaths, as the crowds cheered them on.

Bullfight in Seville

We returned home after Seville, weary but happy and enlightened, after seeing how so many people live their different cultures, yet strive for the same things in life that makes life so worthwhile.

Thank you, Mom, wherever you are. You gave us a great gift . . . a chance to see a world, different, but in many ways the same as the life we live in our country. You provided David and me with a chance to enjoy each other without the responsibility of parenthood. I'm sure the children also enjoyed the break from their parents, and the loving and generous presence of their grandparents.

I became acquainted with Murphy and his law early in life. Bumping into him on occasion has prodded me to prove him wrong. And I often have.

MURPHY'S MAYDAY VOYAGE

WHAT HAVE YOU GOT if you take fifty-six boats, add a few doctors and dentists, an accountant and some school teachers then pepper the cruise with a policeman, several dogs, a lawyer, and lots of children? Wait! Sprinkle on a few charter boat skippers and some rookie yachtsmen. You've got a convoy, with a lot of people—some of whom shouldn't even go near a glass of water, *let alone the ocean!*

The annual Piloted Cruise to the Bahamas had attracted yachtsmen to Bahamian waters since the 1950s. The safety factor of crossing the Gulf Stream in a convoy was very comforting to many yachtsmen.

Our adventure on the high seas began on a blistering, hot July morning, in the summer of 1974. Captain Dave (a garment manufacturer) and our sons, mates Cliff (17) and Todd (14), were hard at work fastening the new rubber lifeboat to the deck of our fiberglass boat, *The Cultured Pearl*, a forty-foot Viking yacht fisherman.

I was busy storing the provisions for our two-week trip.

"Did you buy Cheez Doodles?"

"I hope you bought Sprite and not 7UP!"

"Do we have enough toilet paper?"

I wasn't sure who asked what. I yelled, "Yes!"

I was chief cook and bottle-washer. In "nautical terms" . . . I did everything.

My assistant was my daughter, Tina (8). She was also official dog-watcher, in charge of making sure Misty, our Schnauzer, didn't fall overboard.

By 8 a.m., we had readied for departure. A feeling of exhilaration swept the entire family. Though we had enjoyed many short jaunts on our boat, we had never experienced anything like this before.

"All lines secure," yelled Cliff, jumping aboard, as the boat slowly pulled away from the dock.

Our crew of five left Bahia Mar Marina in Fort Lauderdale, Florida, that steamy summer morning, unaware of a sixth member of our crew, MURPHY, who brought his law onboard. *Anything that can go wrong, will go wrong.*

As we picked up speed, to take our position in line with the convoy, the wind lifted the lifeboat, causing its oarlocks to slam the fiberglass deck.

"Todd!" yelled Captain Dave. "Get out there and sit on that !@#?! thing!"

The lifeboat had been secured upside-down instead of right-side-up.

"Great!" Todd shouted, only too happy to relax on the bow of the boat, enjoying the wonderful sea breezes and the invigorating, salty smell of the ocean. The brilliant sun glittered and danced on the water like zillions of fireflies.

While Cliff napped in the cabin below, Tina and I chose to join the captain on the flying bridge. Wind and sea spray in your face are wonderful antidotes for seasickness!

Many fishing boats have two control stations for steering. The lower station is, generally, inside the cabin; the flying bridge is above, often open for better visibility and fresh air. Besides . . . on a clear day you can see forever!

About an hour out, our engine alarm went off. The starboard engine was overheating.

"*The Cultured Pearl* in need of assistance!" Captain Dave repeated twice on our ship's radio.

The mechanic travelling with the convoy heard our call for help. He pulled alongside our boat, but the seas had begun to pitch as he tried, with difficulty, to board. Fortunately, he was able to board, and discovered it was only a faulty sensor. Breathing a sigh of relief, we continued on our way. The mechanic remained on board for an hour more.

"The weather's turning," I mentioned to Captain Dave. I had prayed for good weather for the crossing; the Gulf Stream was no piece of cake.

Huge black clouds began to form, encircling the convoy like a giant lasso. The boat pitched and swayed. The seas turned up to ten feet at times, making it difficult to move around.

Then, the rains came. This was the first of three squalls we would encounter in the next few hours. The temperature dropped suddenly and the chilling wetness engulfed us.

"Todd!" I screamed. We had almost forgotten he was still sitting on the lifeboat. "He'll be washed overboard!"

I slid down the ladder to the aft deck and crawled on my hands and knees into the cabin. I pulled out some rope and a sweatshirt. It was like riding a bronco. I held on for dear life as I made my way to the bow of the boat. Todd was struggling to hold on.

"Am I glad to see you!" he said, as I tied him to the boat.

"Hold on, Todd, I'm sure it won't last much longer." My heart was heavy as I slowly crept back.

"Mayday! Mayday!" I heard the call on the radio as I reached the flying bridge. This was the signal for help from another boat. The convoy, divided into three groups according to speed, had an assist boat in each group. We were the assist boat in our group.

Leaving our position, we went to the aid of a smaller, older, wooden boat that had sprung a leak and had begun to take on water. We remained until the mechanic was able to repair the leak. With grateful farewells, we again took up our position.

An hour later, the storm eased—enough that I could make my way back to the cabin. I woke Cliff.

"Let me sleep," Cliff muttered, trying to pull the covers over his head. I pulled the blankets off and he stared at me—unaware of anything that had happened, even the storm.

He quickly dressed, apologizing for leaving Todd on his own during the storm. "I'm really sorry, Mom. He must be a drowned rat by now, and I know one of us has to keep the lifeboat from cracking the hull. I'll sit on it till we reach port."

The boys exchanged places. Todd's lips were blue and his teeth chattered. I peeled off his wet clothes like a banana, and tucked him under the covers in the bunk bed. He quickly fell asleep from exhaustion.

The storm picked up again. The ten-foot waves hit the boat, sending heavy sea spray over the top of the flying bridge. *When would it end?* I prayed that Cliff could hold on.

Our boat stabilized after a while and I realized that the storm had subsided. The darkness slowly lifted and the sun began a game of peek-a-boo.

"Mayday! Mayday!" came across the radio.

"Not again!" said Captain Dave. We listened for the name and position of the boat—then headed in its direction.

Smoke was rising from the cabin as we approached. One of the engines had caught fire and the crew was desperately trying to extinguish it. Again, we remained until help arrived, as the mechanic had remained on board with the older, wooden boat that had sprung a leak.

Finally, the clouds dispersed and drifted away. The warmth of the sun felt so good!

"Hurray!" yelled our crew, as we spotted land. Everyone was anxious after the long, rough voyage.

A smaller boat—impatient to reach shore—sped up and passed a slower motor yacht, creating bumpy waves. A little Dachshund was sitting on a cushion on the aft deck of the larger boat. The sudden motion of the boat threw him overboard.

The Cultured Pearl to the rescue! We were directly behind the motor yacht and had seen what had happened. We slowed almost to a stop. Cliff yelled, "I'll get the fishing net!" As I held his legs, Cliff leaned over the side of the boat, and scooped up the frightened dog with the net. We pulled alongside the other boat and, with great difficulty, managed to hand over the dog to its owners.

When our yacht finally entered Lucayan Harbour, on Grand Bahama Island, we were a weary but happy crew. We gleefully agreed: THROW MURPHY OVERBOARD.

After a delightful two days of relaxation, we set our course for the next island on our itinerary, Great Harbour Cay. The weather was magnificent and the seas were calm. From that point on, it was smooth sailing.

The *Cultured Pearl,* on its way to join the annual Piloted Cruise to the Bahamas, July, 1974

Part Two
THE MIDDLE YEARS & BEYOND

Share adventures with your children when they're young. They will cherish the memories forever.

AFTER MY TWO SONS were born, I knew I could not stop until I had a daughter; Tina was my fifth pregnancy. After a miscarriage and an ectopic pregnancy, in which I was told five years later that I had lost a girl, I finally gave birth to Tina. I lived with the adage, "Never say never." When she was born everyone knew her name without having to ask, as I had the name selected for the previous ten years. But all was not well. Tina was born four weeks early and did not have a fully matured digestive system. Within a week of bringing her home from the hospital she had lost weight and complications had set in. The doctor advised me to hire a nurse to wake her every four hours throughout the night, and feed her with an eyedropper, till she could be fed with a bottle. She thrived. My daughter holds a very special place in my heart.

Tina had an advantage, being six and nine years younger than her two brothers; they were in college when we decided to embark on an exciting birthday trip with her. Being the only child left at home, she shared many of the benefits of being an only child, including special time with her parents.

Tina's birthday, which is in April, coincided with her spring break from school. We decided to celebrate her thirteenth birthday in Israel. She had not studied for a bat mitzvah, but David was going to say the prayers at the Western Wall, which would have given her that honor. Unfortunately, a week before our trip, a bomb exploded in the King David Hotel, where we would be staying, and our family called us with great concerns. We wanted to make it a special birthday, so we asked a friend, who was a travel agent, to prepare a trip that Tina would never forget. Tina often reminisces about her trip, although it was more than thirty years ago. My only regret was that we didn't have the opportunity to share the same experience with my boys when they were young.

TINA'S THIRTEENTH BIRTHDAY TRIP: 1979

WE ARRIVED IN ROME at what would be the start of a whirlwind adventure; we wanted to share with Tina many of the sites of this great city that we loved. We began with the Coliseum, one of the most famous monuments of ancient Rome. Tina envisioned the gladiator competitions that took place there: "Just like in the movies," she commented.

A day at the Coliseum

The Trevi Fountain, was a fun visit for Tina. The tradition is to throw a coin into the fountain and make a wish. The coin-toss is said to ensure a return to Rome. Tina stood for a while, with her eyes closed, before throwing her coin. Her wish must have been a *really* good one. She asked for more coins, because she had three more wishes to make. Some of the scenes in the 1953 film *Roman Holiday*, starring Audrey Hepburn and Gregory Peck, were filmed at the Trevi Fountain. I'd love to rent that movie when Tina comes to visit me someday, and see her reaction. She never told me her wishes, but I hope they all came true.

We shared our wonderful experience of the Piazza Navona with Tina, having lunch on the Piazza at Tre Scalini, and enjoyed the famous ice cream, tartufo, that David and I had loved. We all indulged this time with gusto! She wanted to have it every night while in Rome.

Tina was introduced to her first opera, *Madame Butterfly*, at the famous Rome Opera House. She was mesmerized, and asked if we would take her to see it again in New York. Opera added another dimension to her love of music. Watching her sweet, young face light up with every new experience made this adventure, perhaps, even more thrilling for us than for her.

On the Sunday before we left Rome we drove out of the city on the Appian Way to lunch at Sora Rosa. This wonderful restaurant sits outside the city and is renowned for its "pressed chicken." We lunched under the shade of a tree, enjoying the cool, but beautiful weather and the delicious food. Our waiter informed us that the gentleman dining at the next table was the president of Italy.

Sunday lunch at Sora Rosa on the Appian Way

We laughed our way through Europe. I recall a silly game that David adopted. Whenever he saw a phone booth on the street, he picked up the phone, without dialing, and said, "Sorry! No one's home." Tina followed in her father's footsteps and picked up every phone in sight, repeating the same message. She continued the routine after returning home in New York City, till I had to put a stop to it.

The next day we took the train to Florence. Again, we shared the wonderful sites of this historic city with Tina, introducing her to an outstanding world of art at the Uffizi and the Pitti Palace. The food in Florence was fantastic and Tina became an aficionado of great Italian cuisine, especially pasta. She developed a love for cooking in later years, which she attributes to her early exposure to some of the great dishes she remembered as a child in Europe.

Two days later, we continued on to Venice, and were told that Venice, with its myriad of canals, had been sinking for many years. Fortunately, it's still there today. When we took our boat trip on the gondola, our gondolier sang to us as he paddled his way through the canals. Tina reciprocated and sang a song to the gondolier. He loved it! To

**Tina sitting for her portrait
In the square in Florence**

this day, after Tina has travelled much of the world, Venice remains one of her favorite cities. After three days of Venetian hospitality and dining we finally said farewell to Italy and left for Paris.

Tina entertaining the Italian Navy in Venice

When we arrived in Paris, Tina wanted to go to the Eiffel Tower before visiting any other site. We decided to have lunch at the top of the tower before viewing the city through the large telescopes along the railings.

We stepped outside at the top of the tower and Tina quickly went to view the city from the telescope resting against the railing. My acrophobia suddenly kicked in, and I couldn't leave the inner wall of the tower. I called to Tina to please come away from the edge, but my fearless daughter remained at the railing enjoying the breathtaking view of Paris. I still remember her shouting back, "I'm fine Mom, what's the problem?"

Tina viewing the city of Paris

On Easter Sunday we boarded Le Bateau for a delightful trip on the River Seine. Some of the most beautiful monuments in Paris, among them the Eiffel Tower, the Louvre and Notre Dame Cathedral, can be viewed while relaxing aboard Le Bateau. Afterwards, we went to the Left Bank to a recommended restaurant for our favorite desert, *tarte tatin*. We enjoyed this delicious apple tart every day while in Paris . . . sometimes twice a day. Tina made me promise I would learn how to make it when we went home. And I did.

Tina also got to experience her second opera, *La bohème*, at the famous Paris Opera. To this day, she claims it's her favorite opera. After seeing it again in New York City she still ranks the Paris performance as the best. Exposing Tina, at an early age, to a classical music world, I believe enriched her appreciation of all music. Seeing and listening to the sights and sounds through the eyes of our thirteen-year-old daughter, I believe gave us a different perspective of all we had seen and heard before. Travelling with her was a pure delight; her enthusiasm and laughter were contagious.

The last stop on our sojourn brought us to London. We attempted to show Tina every site we could in the time remaining. She loved the ceremony of "Changing the Guard" at Buckingham Palace. The pomp and formality of the Queen's regiment is always impressive, and she wanted to be part of it.

Tina sharing the duties of the sentry at Buckingham Palace

Tina's thirteenth birthday, April 18th, arrived a few days before returning home from London. Her birthday wish was to see the show, *Tommy*, a rock opera by The Who, one of her favorite rock groups. Theater in London began earlier than in New York. David made arrangements with the Connaught Hotel for a private, birthday dinner at 5:30 p.m., an hour before the restaurant at the hotel opened to the public. There were three waiters, waiting on "Princess Tina," to serve her every need. The smile never left her young face. She experienced dining on beef Wellington and chocolate soufflé for the first time. She has often said, "This was my favorite birthday dinner . . . EVER!"

The entire trip was everything we wanted to share with her and expose her to. I believe the trip matured her in ways that could not have been accomplished by travelling with the entire family at home in the USA. I saw a change in her demeanor as she entered her teenage years. A few years later, when she travelled to Europe on a teen tour, and then with her school, she had a more sophisticated appreciation of travelling abroad.

This trip has lived among her cherished memories throughout her life, and we still reminisce about that exciting trip.

Never lose your sense of humor. You can often find humor in many situations if you look for it. If you don't have a sense of humor . . . find one. It will help you live longer and happier.

I ENJOYED SHOPPING WITH my husband, except when it came to the supermarket and David came armed with coupons. He delighted in filling the basket with products I never heard of and couldn't use, but he had the coupon and the expiration date was near. When we got to the check-out counter the faces of the shoppers behind us made me want to race for the front door. He often submitted twelve to fifteen coupons. His face lit up when he saw the savings. I wasn't a happy camper. He really enjoyed the adventure and found it very funny. I didn't. I returned many of the products when he wasn't with me. I wrote this story in the mid 1980s, and still chuckle when I remember David's expression when he read it. He didn't see it the way I did, but he loved my humor. Many of these products no longer exist today, but they had great names for telling a humorous tale.

THE COUPON ADDICT

FIVE BOTTLES OF MURPHY OIL SOAP, six bottles of Pine Sol, four Fantastik! Lestoil, Spic and Span, Mr. Clean, Top Job, followed by Tough Act and Simple Green. *Simple Green?* The supply is endless. Is my husband trying to tell me something?

X-14 Mildew Remover? It sounds like a secret weapon.

One week my carpets smell like spiced apples, the next week, cinnamon sticks. The scent of peach blossom and country berry permeate the air in the following weeks—compliments of Glade.

I'm married to an addict. Dave doesn't drink, smoke, gamble or do drugs—he's really a sweet guy. But, don't feed him coupons and let him loose in a supermarket; the addiction takes over.

Our grocery bills are enormous, but . . . noooo, Dave says, "Look how much we're saving!"

Fifty-four 100-watt, long-life light bulbs. DOES ANYBODY NEED FIFTY-FOUR LONG-LIFE LIGHT BULBS?!? We could light up America!

I brush my teeth six times a day, trying to stay ahead of the next supply of toothpaste.

Sixty-two rolls of toilet paper . . . I pray for diarrhea; I've run out of storage space.

Imagine . . . 2000 Flushes! My toilet bowls match my wardrobe: 2000 Blue, 2000 Green, Lavender Bloo, and Crystal Clear—it goes with everything.

I hide the coupons from the Sunday papers, and the ones we receive in the mail. Somehow, Dave finds more.

My laundry . . . oh, my laundry. First, I Shout it out. Then, I'm Bold as I go it Solo. Yes! Yes! I Cheer--the Dynamo that I am--as I Wisk it away and end it All. Then . . . I Snuggle up to it.

I've got Scrunges and Spiffits, Dusters and Spruce-Ups. Touch-Ups, Wipe-Ups, Clean-Ups—why am I down when I could be so up?

Dave should be home soon. I hope he didn't forget the milk and the eggs.

Turtles, Lucky Charms, Trix, Cocoa Puffs, Fruity Pebbles—what ever happened to good old Rice Krispies? At least I have a good cup of coffee in the morning, with my Folgers, Maxwell House, Taster's Choice, Nescafé mixture.

I've got Magic Mushrooms in my bathrooms (how psychedelic)—no mushrooms in the kitchen. No coupon.

Dave's home. Oh, no . . . look at those bundles!

"Hi, honey! I got some great buys tonight. They have double coupons this week. I saved $21.65."

"What's this? PAMPERS?!? Dave, we don't have kids in diapers anymore!"

"I use them to wash the car."

"Where's the milk and the eggs?"

"Sorry, honey, you'll pick it up tomorrow."

"But, I need them tomorrow morning."

"You wouldn't want me to go back in this storm. Hear the thunder? Wait . . . what's this in my pocket? Two coupons for Ziploc bags—they expire today. I'll be back in twenty minutes."

Inspiration can be a noble and stimulating emotion. Just be careful where you use it.

WATCH WHERE YOU'RE GOING WITH THOSE GREAT IDEAS!

MY IDEA SWITCH SEEMS to be broken; I can't turn it off. Especially at 3:30 in the morning. I'm always writing in my head. On paper? Well, that's a different story.

Make sure your feet, your hands and your head are firmly planted when your mind decides to travel to a faraway time and place.

Recently, I was driving to Long Island from New York City for an appointment with my gynecologist. As I passed LaGuardia Airport, the opposing traffic was stalled because of an accident. I watched two children battling in the back of a station wagon while the distraught mother sat at the wheel. My radio was tuned to a talk show discussing sibling rivalry.

Immediately, the wheels of my mental writing machine went into full gear. Minutes later, after making an automatic turn onto another highway, I became completely disoriented. Actually, I was headed in the right direction, but for a few moments, I was completely lost. I didn't know where I was or where I was going. I pulled over to the side of the road. Could I have travelled to such depths of a story? Apparently, I had.

I pulled back onto the road after realizing I was headed in the right direction and continued on. *Phew!* That was REALLY scary. My heart was pounding. Never again, I promised myself. There is a time and a place for everything. Jotting in my mind's notebook is fine, but writing the final draft, in a precarious situation, can be *hazardous* to your health.

The following is my current "do and don't" list for mental writing:

1) Do write while listening to a Mahler symphony in Avery Fisher Hall at Lincoln Center. *Safe.*
2) Do write while watching *Barney and the Backyard Gang* for the forty-seventh time with your two-year-old grandson.
3) Do write while listening to your friend on the telephone describe, in detail, the latest news about her granddaughter. How she eats, sleeps and breathes at the age of eight months.
4) Don't write while racing down the steps of Madison Square Garden after a basketball game. *Definitely dangerous.*
5) Don't write while crossing the intersection of 42ndStreet and Broadway in New York City at rush hour. *Watch out!*

6) Don't write while walking your dog. You never know what you might step in.

7) Definitely write down those great ideas on a plane trip. No telephones, no doorbells, no housekeeping, no laundry, no interruptions . . . unless the stewardess announces, "Fasten your seatbelts, please. We'll be making an emergency landing." Long bus, train and car rides will also suffice . . . as long as you're not at the wheel.

The land of Israel draws one like a magnet. Israel and the Palestinian territories comprise the major part of the Holy Land. It has been sacred to the Jewish people since Biblical times, but is important to people of all Abrahamic religions—Jews, Christians and Muslims.

THE LAND OF ISRAEL

IN THE SUMMER OF 1985, my husband, David, was chosen to be the honoree for the apparel industry's gala dinner in New York City for the American Committee for Shaare Zedek Medical Center in Jerusalem. Through his persistence and efforts he was able to raise hundreds of thousands of dollars for this incredible hospital.

Shaare Zedek Medical Center is an enormous complex serving the entire population of Jerusalem, both Israelis and Palestinians. The hospital maintains offices around the world. The construction of Shaare Zedek, the most modern hospital in the Middle East, was completed in 1902; it has become a legend throughout the world.

In 1979, Shaare Zedek moved to the new, ultra-modern Medical Center. In 1985 the Ethiopian immigrants arrived, in full force, through "Operation Moses," and were treated for tropical diseases. A special department was then opened for tropical diseases. The operating rooms are underground, so wartime or terror attacks or other such disturbances aboveground don't interrupt surgery.

The hospital has almost every department needed to treat patients with specific diseases. It has an excellent neonatal department and has formed a separate unit for children, consolidating the different departments involved in pediatric medicine.

As of this writing, Shaare Zedek is treating tsunami victims in Japan with IDF (Israel Defense Forces) relief.

David and I arrived in Jerusalem in October 1985. We were met at the airport and taken directly to the hospital. We donned surgical gowns and were taken on a tour of the hospital. During the tour, we filmed a documentary to be shown back in New York City.

I was overwhelmed by this incredible hospital. Each department was so specialized; it was like visiting several hospitals in one. I can never forget the tiniest baby I ever saw, lying in an incubator. It was born weighing only 1 lb. 8 oz., and thriving. I felt so proud and honored to be a part of supporting the

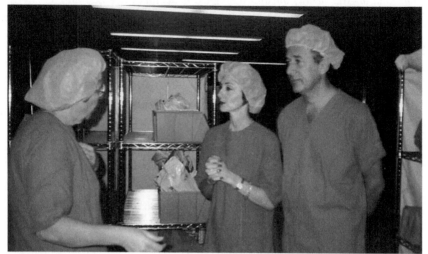

Preparing for our hospital tour of Shaare Zedek

wonderful work that this hospital does, and offers not only to the people of Jerusalem, but to all of Israel. I had the opportunity to speak to a Palestinian mother. With tears in her eyes, she said, "They saved the life of my son. They are so good to us here. I love this place."

I thought to myself, *why can't all the people of Israel feel this way, and get along? They all share the same origin.* When John Lennon wrote his inspiring song, "Imagine," he had a beautiful vision of world peace. The words of that song are haunting. The world would achieve a great lesson by adopting the words to his song.

After our first day at the hospital, we began our tour of Israel. There were so many sights to see, I felt I was going back in time. Jerusalem is a magical city. It is a unique combination of ancient history, spiritual sanctity and many cultures.

We visited the Tower of David, an ancient citadel located near the Jaffa Gate entrance to the Old City of Jerusalem. It was constructed during the second century B.C.E., then destroyed and rebuilt. It's amazing how much of the citadel remains today.

We went to the Arab Market, where one could buy almost anything. It reminded me of our flea markets back home.

The Western Wall (Wailing Wall) affected me deeply. It is a remnant of the ancient wall that surrounded the Jewish Temple's courtyard. Next to the Temple Mount it is one of the most sacred sites in Judaism. A wrought iron fence divides the women's side from the men's side. I promised myself I

The Tower of David

would not cry when I touched the wall. I had a few notes to tuck into the cracks in the wall, as is the tradition. I had been working with terminally ill children in a volunteer program in a New York City hospital. I fell in love with a three-year-old boy patient and wanted to leave his name in this sacred wall. People place their prayers and wishes into the wall, in the hope that they will come true. When I placed my hand upon the wall, I broke down and began to sob. The young and old alike were leaning their heads against the wall, silently praying and weeping. I have never visited a site anywhere in my travels that created such heart-wrenching emotions.

When David met me after we left the wall, I saw the tears in his eyes. We couldn't speak for the first few moments.

The Western Wall

One's first visit to Jerusalem is a very emotional one. There is so much history here. A private tour of Yad Vashem, the Holocaust Museum, was arranged for us. Years later, I visited the Holocaust Museum in Washington. Yad Vashem had left me emotionally drained, and again I relived the horrors of this tragic period.

After Jerusalem, we continued on a fascinating tour of Israel. Standing atop Masada, I was mesmerized by its history. Masada is a great symbol for the Jewish people. Israeli soldiers take an oath there: "Masada shall not fall again."

Ancient palaces and fortifications were built atop this rocky plateau. It rests isolated in the South District of Israel on the eastern edge of the Judean Desert, overlooking the Dead Sea. I urge everyone to research the history of this incredible place.

Standing atop Masada overlooking the Dead Sea

After leaving Masada, we visited the Dead Sea. David went into the water, but swimming was difficult; this was due to the fact that the Dead Sea is a salt lake, one of the world's saltiest bodies of water. Floating on top was very relaxing. The sea borders Jordan to the east and Israel and the West Bank to the west.

Our trip took us next on a visit to a kibbutz near Lake Tiberias. Later that day, we lunched at a restaurant overlooking the lake. I ate the most delicious fish called St. Peter's Fish, which is similar to—if not the same as— John Dory, which is available in some restaurants back in New York. Whenever I see it on the menu, that's my choice.

Before the end of our trip, our group planned to visit Dr. Gisella Perl, who lived in Herzliya, a city not far from Tel Aviv, in the north of Israel. Gisella Perl was a Jewish gynecologist who lived in Romania (at the time it was part of Hungary), when in 1944 the Nazis invaded Hungary and deported its Jewish population.

We had planned to continue on into Europe, visiting a few cities we had never been to before. I was so disappointed that we were not able to be part of the group that was travelling to Herzliya to visit Dr. Perl, as we were leaving when their visit was planned. As a kind gesture, Dr. Perl's sister came to visit with David and me at our hotel, and shared so many stories about her sister and their lives. Dr. Perl's sister was one of the lucky ones, as she had departed Hungary before the Nazis arrived and had migrated to Israel. She gave me a gift of Dr. Perl's book. I read the entire book on the trip home from Europe. And I cried all the way. Her sister related the following story of the horrendous events of Dr. Perl's tragic experience.

Gisella Perl was deported to Auschwitz, along with her family. Her husband, her son and her parents and other relatives were exterminated in the camps. She worked as a doctor in the camp and saved the lives of hundreds of pregnant women by secretly aborting their pregnancies with her bare hands. There were no antiseptics available, or even running water, or medical instruments. Pregnant women were either killed or used by Dr. Josef Mengele for experiments.

In 1948 she published her story in a book, *I Was A Doctor in Auschwitz*. She died in 1988. In 2003, Christine Lahti starred in a film, *Out of the Ashes*, a story based upon the life of Dr. Perl.

Our visit to Israel was over too quickly. We vowed to return soon and we did. In 1987 we returned with a group of the American Committee for Shaare Zedek Hospital.

AFTER DEPARTING ISRAEL, we went to Vienna, Budapest, Munich and London, before returning home.

Vienna is called the "City of Music"; some of the most famous composers lived there. We enjoyed a thrilling concert at the Vienna Philharmonic.

Arriving in Budapest, I discovered that this city was actually two cities on either side of the river. One side was Buda, the other side was Pest. Budapest became a single city, occupying both banks of the Danube River, in November, 1873.

Buda and Pest sides of Budapest on the Danube River

We hired a wonderful guide to show us the highlights of Budapest and its surroundings. Peter was a fascinating man who shared with us incredible stories of World War II in his homeland. Although he was not Jewish, he was involved with the synagogue and took us to visit the magnificent synagogue of Budapest. Behind the building is a garden devoted to the "Righteous Gentiles" who saved the lives of Jews during the war, including his father.

Atop the city of Budapest with our guide Peter

Resting at a memorial in Budapest

After Budapest we left for Munich. The weather had turned quite cool. We planned on going to the Dachau concentration camp outside the city, but it was already the end of October. The concierge at the hotel suggested we cancel the trip, as the tour buses had stopped running the previous week. He told us it might be difficult to get a taxi to return to the city. I can't imagine being stranded at Dachau! Years later, in Poland, I visited Auschwitz and Birkenau. That was enough for me. I'm glad we never got to Dachau.

Thomas Mann, the German novelist and short story writer, lived in Munich until he was driven out of the city by the Nazis because of his religion. Today, we found the German people to be warm and friendly, especially toward Americans.

The last stop was London . . . a favorite of ours. We tried to make it a habit of stopping in London for a few days before returning to the States. It is the shortest trip home from any place in Europe, and we loved the London theater.

The addition to our trip to Israel was enjoyable, but Israel was memorable. *I left my heart there.* It was beyond anything I had imagined. Friends had related their stories and love of Israel, but until you visit Israel yourself, you cannot appreciate this awe-inspiring country.

"Next year in Jerusalem" is a familiar phrase. Once having visited this historic city, the urge to return remains strong.

ISRAEL REVISITED

OUR RETURN TO ISRAEL occurred on April 27th, 1987. We travelled with a group of the American Committee for Shaare Zedek Hospital.

From the moment I stepped off the plane, the exhilarating emotion that I felt when visiting Israel in 1985 returned.

The trip, this time, took us beyond the areas we had visited before. I felt I had not seen enough of this magnificent country, in which the Israelis had turned a desert into a garden. The history of this country came alive with our guide, No-No. His story-telling brought us back in time. No-No was a seventh-generation sabra, a very large man, and a former rabbi, who now guided people throughout his country. No-No was James Michener's guide when he travelled through Israel and wrote his book, *The Source*.

The day after we arrived, we departed Jerusalem and travelled through Judea and Samaria to one of the new settlements, where we met with the residents.

We continued touring, and after a picnic lunch we were met by a Lieutenant Colonel of the Israeli Defense Force. We were given a briefing on the northern frontier security situation.

We then drove to the capital of the Lower Galilee, Tiberias, and checked into the Jordan River Hotel. In the evening we boarded a boat for dinner and a cruise on Lake Tiberias, also known as the Sea of Galilee. We joined in the folk dancing and singing aboard the boat, which created a festive atmosphere of this special evening. The Israelis love their music and live their lives to the fullest, knowing how fragile their existence is.

Two years earlier, when we had visited Shaare Zedek, we became friendly with a wonderful woman who was the social director of the hospital. She planned all the events we enjoyed. I loved listening to her stories and how she came to live in Israel from South Africa. She told us that when she moved to Israel when her children were younger and in their teenage years, her son's close friend was a Palestinian boy. One day, when he was about nineteen years old, he went to his friend's house, as he often did, and was told by the friend's mother that he could no longer associate with her son. That was the beginning of the "divide." Until that point, everyone lived together amicably. I was very saddened by that story.

The following day we met with a representative of the Kiryat Shmona Municipality. He guided us through the health center. We met with the medical staff and heard about emergency assistance and care, a very important part of Israel's medical services.

We visited with the children and heard about the difference in their lives from the children living in other safer parts of Israel. Bunkers and bomb shelters were an integral part of their existence.

The children of Kiryat Shmona

Kiryat Shmona is Israel's northernmost, smallest city, located in the upper Galilee close to the Lebanon border. One-third of its population is younger than nineteen. The close location to Lebanon makes it a target for rocket fire cross-border attacks.

In the spring of 1974, three members of the Popular Front for the Liberation of Palestine crossed the border

Memorial Park—Kiryat Shmona

from Lebanon, and massacred eighteen residents, including children.

We left Kiryat Shmona and proceeded to ascend the Golan Heights. We travelled past the former Syrian positions overlooking the Galilee, and the former Syrian army headquarters.

The valleys of Israel—from wasteland to farmland

The Golan is strategically important to Israel in preventing its defense from being overrun and allowing Arab armies to flood the country. The Golan is only sixty miles long—without any major terrain obstacles—from the western Golan to Haifa and Acre. It extends between the borders of Lebanon, Jordan and Syria, overlooking the Hula Valley, Israel's richest agricultural area. If controlled by a hostile country, like Syria, the Golan becomes a major threat to the security of Israel. Afterwards, we were guests of an armored unit on the Golan and lunched with the officers and soldiers.

Returning to Jerusalem, we stopped to visit Haifa, a modern port city overlooking the Mediterranean, nestled in the mountains. Much of Israel's high technology research and industry is located here.

Continuing on to Jerusalem we visited a great Crusades city: Ceasarea. The city was built by Herod the Great. It was once the seat of Roman rule; Roman and Crusades ruins and the ancient aqueduct still exist today.

The following day was spent at Shaare Zedek Hospital, listening to lectures and discussions about the medical procedures at the hospital. We also spent time with the children in the Pediatric Ward, and were introduced to unique features of the medical center. I loved watching both Arab and Jewish children playing together in the playroom.

After lunch, we participated in a private wreath laying ceremony in the Memorial Hall at Yad Vashem. We toured the museum and walked along the Avenue of the Righteous.

On Friday, May 1st, we took a full day tour of Jerusalem. We walked through many quarters of the Old City, seeing the Christian, Muslim and Reconstructed Jewish Quarter. We enjoyed shopping in the Arab markets; they were very gracious and welcoming to their American guests.

In the evening we shared a traditional Shabbat dinner in the reconstructed Chabad House in the Old City. The evening was spirited, unlike anything I had ever attended. The rabbi was quite young and had a beautiful, young Russian wife. He toasted our entourage about seven times, slugging down the straight, strong whiskey, encouraging the men to the same. The men were a little unstable, but smiling, when we got up to leave and stumbled back to the hotel.

On Saturday evening we joined the residents of Jerusalem at the Western Wall for the opening ceremonies of Memorial Day. David returned to the wall. Again, he was so emotionally moved, but he wanted to express his appreciation of all his blessings.

David at the Western Wall

Sunday, May 3rd, was Memorial Day. We departed very early for Masada. Though we had visited Masada two years earlier, somehow the story our guide related to us this time brought Masada more alive. Masada remains the symbol of bravery and freedom for modern-day Israel.

Masada held out for three years against the legions of Flavius Silva and chose death in preference to Roman slavery. The spirit of the defenders of Masada remains today in these words, "We shall not be slaves. We will be free."

We continued on, visiting the Biblical city of Arad, a town in the middle of the Negev, and then went to Beersheva (also known as Beersheba), the capital of the Negev. Beersheva has been known since Abraham's time, and today is a modern, thriving university city.

Our travels took us to Tel Aviv on Sunday evening. We celebrated Independence Day with the local residents of Tel Aviv.

In the morning, while driving south to the industrial town of Ashdod, Ashkelon and Kibbutz Yad Mordechai, the horns were blowing all over Israel to commemorate Independence Day. All cars stopped on the road for a moment of silence. Everyone left their vehicles and stepped out onto the edge of the road, bowed their heads, and then continued on.

When we arrived at the kibbutz, we saw a constructed battle scene depicting the siege on the settlement by the Egyptian Army during the War of Independence.

We went next to Moshav Netiv Ha'asara. Here, former settlers of Yamit, the town dismantled as a result of the Camp David Peace Agreement, are turning the desert into a beautiful garden.

The Hapoel Games in Tel Aviv

In the evening we attended the opening ceremonies of the Hapoel Games. Participants from all over the world compete in this great sporting event. The games include more than twenty branches of sport. Among some of the sports are gymnastics, swimming, wrestling, fencing, soccer, football, tennis, and even bridge and chess.

On Tuesday, May 5th, our last day in Israel, we visited the Diaspora Museum and saw a presentation of more than two thousand years of Jewish history and heritage.

Our last visit was Jaffa. This ancient port city is the home of many artisan studios and small art shops. Late that evening, we headed to Ben Gurion Airport for our flight home.

Israel is an awe-inspiring country that I have been fortunate to visit twice in my many travels. It remains a true human experience. My greatest wish is for all the people of Israel to live together in peace. They have so much to share and to learn from one another.

SHORTLY AFTER RETURNING HOME, we attended a Shaare Zedek Hospital dinner in New York City to honor Raoul Wallenberg, the Swedish humanitarian. Wallenberg worked in Budapest, Hungary, during World War II and rescued tens of thousands of Jewish lives, by issuing protective passports and housing Jews in buildings established as Swedish territory.[1]

Congressman Tom Lantos was among those saved, and in 1981 he sponsored a bill making Wallenberg an Honorary Citizen of the United States.[2]

The Raoul Wallenberg Award is periodically bestowed on a select number of people, organizations and committees whose courage and selflessness against great odds personify those traits of Raoul Wallenberg.[3]

Talking to H. Ross Perot—He received the Raoul Wallenberg Award at the dinner, for his personal courage in the dramatic rescue of his American employees being held captive in Iran.

Be grateful for all the good you receive and be very giving in return. One of the best ways to give back is to give to the future; children are the future.

I HAD ALWAYS WANTED TO volunteer and work with children. Living on Long Island, I once offered my services as a volunteer at a nearby hospital. The head of Volunteer Services appreciated my offer, but after our interview suggested that I wait a few years. My children were still young, and she explained that I was needed as a volunteer on a steady basis. She felt that when one had young children at home, a parent wasn't always dependable, especially if children were at home sick. She was right; I had three children with severe allergies, and throughout the winters there was usually one child at home sick almost every week. Shortly after that, we moved to Florida.

We moved back to Long Island, NY, in the mid-seventies and became involved in building a weekend house in Connecticut. I waited for the time to come when I could finally fulfill my desire to volunteer working with children. In 1984, when we moved into Manhattan, I was in walking distance of New York University Hospital. The time was ripe. My youngest child was now in college.

The Director of Volunteers at New York University Hospital was warm and charming; the interview was quite lengthy. She asked me what I would like to do as a volunteer in the pediatric department. When I told her about the stories I wrote for children and enjoyed reading to my own children, she was very enthusiastic. She suggested I work with the children's librarian and create a reading hour for young patients . . . and I did. Almost every Monday, for five years, I read to, played with, and made up stories to share with the children.

When I began my volunteer work (it was called a Therapeutic Recreational Program) I wasn't prepared for the emotional roller coaster I would be riding. Many of the children on the ward were terminally ill with cancer. Some of the children had undergone brain surgeries, and their little shaved heads had stitches running across the top of their heads like mini railroad tracks. When I left for the hospital each Monday morning, my heart was light with anticipation for the day ahead. Returning home, at the end of the day, my heart was very heavy. Mondays became the most emotionally difficult day of the week for me.

The children loved and looked forward to our reading hour. Many children remained at the hospital for weeks, thus strong bonds and relationships often developed between us. They sat in a circle on the floor in front of me, some begging to sit on my lap, even two at a time.

One morning, after a story session, seven-year-old Jenny waved her arm, stood up, and said, "When I grow up, I want to write just like you, and tell stories to children."

"Great, Jenny! And what about you, Jason?"

"I don't know."

"What do you want to be, Liz? And Michael and Scottie?"

"I don't know," was the answer from almost all the children.

Then Jenny got up and said, "Write us a story about when we grow up."

I loved that little Jenny. Despite all the chemo she endured, because of her brain cancer, she had more vitality for life than many grownups. Most of the children in my group suffered life-threatening illnesses. I learned that children are among the bravest people on earth.

I promised the children I would write the story and read it the following Monday. This is the story I wrote for the children.

WHO AM I?

I'M SEVEN YEARS OLD and I'm Penny's big brother. She's only three. I wanted a little brother when she was born. When my mom went to the hospital, I told my dad, "If you bring home a girl I'll throw her out!" But, I didn't.

I love her most of the time—except when she grabs my toys and breaks them. And I hate her sticky, lollipop fingers all over my books. But, she's really funny. She makes me laugh a lot when she dresses herself and puts her clothes on backwards.

My brother, Allan, is ten. So, I'm a little brother, too. Sometimes, Allan is mean. But, I love him. He takes me with him to play with his friends and takes me to the movies. He taught me to throw a softball and he helps me with my homework.

My sister, Pat, got married. She's twenty and she's going to have a baby. She's very grown up. She's my half-sister, but she says she loves me "whole."

Pat told me I'm going to be an uncle. I thought uncles were big, like my Uncle Bruce. He's a football player for the Buffalo Bills.

My mom says I'm so good-looking; I look just like my dad. "This is my son," she says when we meet people, and makes me shake hands with everyone.

My dad takes me fishing with his friends. He tells them, "This is my pal." We have a great time together.

When Grandma and Grandpa come to visit, they say I'm the best grandson, because I'm not rowdy and I give them lots of kisses. They never say it in front of Allan, 'cause he'd be jealous.

Mrs. Talbott, my teacher, told me I'm her favorite student. She's so pretty. I think maybe I'll marry her when I grow up.

"You're a very brave patient," says Dr. Davidson. I never cry when he gives me a shot. Well, almost never. The nurse gives me bubblegum if I don't cry. The crybabies get lollipops.

Sometimes, I blow a bubble so big, it bursts in my face and gets stuck to my hair and eyebrows. Mom doesn't like that.

My favorite thing to be is Matt's best friend. Matt and I do everything together. We have swimming races in Matt's pool. He always wins because he's faster than I am. But, when we play ball, I'm a better catcher than Matt, because Allan taught me.

Mom says I'll be many more things by the time I grow up. Maybe I'll be president! She says we play lots of different roles. But, just being me is the most special of all.

I think today I'll just be me, Joey.

How many roles does Joey play?

How many do you?

THE CHILDREN LOVED MY SHORT STORY. They began counting how many roles they played. They tried telling me, many at the same time, all about their brothers and sisters, cousins and friends, grandmas and grandpas, and even neighbors. I was thrilled at the excitement my story generated for the children. Many still didn't know what they wanted to be when they grew up, but they all learned, like Joey, they were very special, and it was good to be just themselves, at least for today. When I left the hospital that day, I prayed that all those children had a future.

After my first grandson was born at the hospital, I ended my five years of volunteering. It was time for me to leave. I knew, sometime in the future, I would return to volunteering with children again.

Fifteen years later, in May of 2006, I was on a plane to Denver, Colorado, for my granddaughter's graduation from high school. Sitting next to a gentleman, we became involved in a conversation about volunteering. He told me about an organization for abused children in which his wife was president of the Fort Lauderdale chapter. His wife was sitting across the aisle from him.

I left my seat and knelt in the aisle next to his wife while she told me about an organization called JAFCO (Jewish Adoption and Foster Care Options). She invited me to visit the children's village after the summer, when I returned to my home in Florida in October. The Children's Village, in Sunrise, Florida, was the home base for JAFCO, where the children lived, safe and protected from physical, emotional and mental abuse.

Her story touched my heart and I knew I was ready to be there, once again, for children in need. The time had come.

I visited the JAFCO Children's Village that fall and I was hooked. I listened to the lecture, watched the film, walked the village and knew this was for me. I became a "godparent," which involved a ten-year financial commitment; but more important, I wanted to spend time with the children.

The village was warm and inviting. There were six beautiful single-family homes; each child received his/her own bedroom and bathroom; boys and girls were separated, and lived with other children close to their own age. Siblings could grow up together. The love and attention these children were given was heart-warming.

The aim of JAFCO is to work together with the family, through counseling, to bring children and their families back together. If that isn't feasible, children can be adopted or placed in foster care, or remain in the village till twenty-one years of age. They go to school from kindergarten through college, and live as normal a life as possible, surrounded by a loving and incredible staff. Their lives are filled with after-school activities, sports, outings, summer camp, holiday festivities, parties and so much more.

I spent a wonderful day with the youngest children, playing with beautiful two-year-old brother and sister twins, and rocking a six-week-old baby in my arms, that had been abandoned by its mother when she walked out of the hospital and away from her newborn. The good news was that the baby had already been adopted by a couple from the Netherlands.

Like my story of Joey, I have lived many roles in my lifetime. I have now assumed another role as "godparent." And I love it!

JAFCO has multiple chapters in South Florida, Philadelphia and New York City.

To quote my husband's college professor, "The mark of a smart man is to know what he doesn't know." Humility plays a large role in defining one's character. It is not always necessary to be "right." It is never necessary to be judgmental.

SOME OF US ARE FAMILIAR with people who "coulda" done it better, "woulda" done it differently, and "shoulda" done it the "right" way. This trait tends to identify *obnoxious* people. The know-it-alls, and the I-could-do-it-betters, are in a class by themselves. In the late 1980s, I attended an elegant party in Manhattan. I was the eavesdropper that evening, and still recall the evening with clarity. I have taken some literary license in the telling of this story: I have changed the identities of the guests, including the celebrities.

WOULDA, COULDA, SHOULDA

"PARTY OF THE YEAR" at the home of Margot and Mel Starr; "cocktails at 6:00 p.m.," read the invitation. Wanda shook her head. "She coulda made it seven . . . especially on a Saturday. Most everyone won't arrive till seven anyhow."

Carol stared at the elegant invitation. "I woulda made the party on Friday. Rush back to the city on the weekend, after soccer and a ten-year-old's birthday party . . . I won't make it till eight."

Sheryl ripped open the gold-edged invitation breathlessly. "Black Tie . . . Party of the Year." Everybody who is anybody will be there. "She'll probably have George Clooney, and I know she's close to Michelle Pfeiffer and her husband, what's-his-name," mumbled Sheryl. "Oh! Margot . . . Margot . . . you shoulda made it Wednesday. You know we're in the city mid-week. I can't make it before nine."

The "Party of the Year" arrived six weeks after its heralded announcement. At 5:45 p.m., the evening of the event, the elevator of the building on posh Park Avenue was filled to capacity every three-and-a-half-minutes—the time it took to leave the lobby and empty out on the penthouse floor.

"Margot! You look ravishing!"

"Margot, darling, the apartment is breathtaking."

"The hors d'oeuvres are fabulous, Margot. I'd love the name of your caterer."

"Is that George Clooney near the window? Margot, you must introduce me."

"You and Mel are the MOST wonderful hosts."

By 6:30 p.m., all the guests had arrived. It was standing room only. Peter Duchin tinkled the ivories of the baby grand piano, as two violinists strolled the apartment, accompanying him with familiar melodies of the 1930s. Itzhak Perlman, an old friend of Margot and Mel's, graciously consented to play a few songs. The sweet strains of the violin prompted Renata Scotto to hum along. Joining in, Peter Duchin turned the threesome into a mini concert. The party was in full swing by 7:00.

An ice sculpture of three penguins, holding platters of caviar, rested in the center of a large table in the galleried hall. Next to it, another ice sculpture of a huge champagne bucket held a dozen bottles of champagne. A third ice sculpture of a crab, about four feet high, presented a display of crab claws, shrimps and raw shellfish. Waiters in white ties and tails carried trays of succulent hors d'oeuvres.

"Wanda!" called Carol, surprised. "I didn't know you would be here this early. I coulda picked you up."

"Sheryl knew . . . she shoulda told you," muttered Wanda through a mouthful of mushroom caps.

Sheryl looked up. "I woulda, but I thought Carol knew."

"GIRLS!" Wanda exclaimed. "Look at that short skirt! She thinks she's twenty-one. She shoulda worn pants . . . what lousy legs."

"What do you think of Margot's facelift, Sheryl?" asked Carol.

"If she went to the surgeon I suggested, in L.A., she woulda had a better job. She coulda gone to anyone."

Two men sat down on the ottoman next to Wanda and proceeded to discuss their golf game.

"Golf! That's the only subject Donald and I have major fights over," moaned Wanda. "We're ready for a divorce whenever we play in a tournament together. He coulda played much better last Sunday and we woulda had a chance to win."

"Same here," Sheryl added. "By the way, how did you score in Wednesday's game? I thought you woulda won."

"I shoulda won, but my partner was terrible. She coulda played much better, too. I needed, *at least*, some help. Why am I always dragged down by everyone else?"

Carol, perusing the room, addressed Wanda, the catering maven.

"Wanda, what do you think of all the ice sculptures? A bit overdone . . . don't you think?"

"I woulda had only one. It takes away from the total effect. The ice bucket woulda been my choice," answered Wanda.

"Do Margot and Mel really know all these celebrities?" asked Sheryl. "I knew George Clooney would be here . . . that's why I came. I wonder if they paid some of them to 'decorate' the party. How *gauche* that would be! I woulda had only one or two celebs."

"I don't know for sure, but I heard Margot might be related to Itzhak Perlman, and she went to school with Michelle . . . I think. I know Mel did business with Peter Duchin. But, you're right . . . it is overkill," added Carol.

"You also can't breathe in here. They shoulda had a smaller gathering. You're really nobody unless you're invited to this party every year. Look around," muttered Sheryl, "I see quite a few nobodies."

Margot and Mel, excellent hosts and renowned party-givers, circulated among their guests, catching tidbits of conversations throughout the apartment.

At 11:00 p.m., guests began to leave, embracing their hosts and extolling and "singing the praises" of the magnificent "party-of-the-year."

Carol, Wanda and Sheryl hugged their hosts and together uttered "FABULOUS!" They expressed their utmost compliments, including the glorious food, the exciting celebrity guests, the wonderful music. Perfection, as usual, in every way. "We can't wait till next year," they exclaimed, and swooshed out the door.

After all the guests had left, Margot smiled and said, " Mel, dear, remind me next time we entertain to eliminate the obnoxious trio."

"Who, dear?"

"Wanda Woulda, Carol Coulda and Sheryl Shoulda."

WHY DID I WRITE THIS NEGATIVE, satirical piece? I have met, perhaps, two people in my life similar to the characters at this party. There are definitely controlling people and those who have an enormous need to be right. But, I have discovered, often, this trait is a result of insecurity. When you have good self-esteem, and are secure in your own judgment, you don't need to prove yourself.

I believe most people have humility and good character. We have to be tolerant and often accepting of those who don't. My wish is that they will learn from those who do.

We often chastise ourselves for the things we *woulda* done differently, *coulda* done better and *shoulda* done if we followed our instincts.

We need to listen to our inner voice and forgive ourselves. We have <u>all</u> made bad choices; wished we could turn back the clock and changed some of the outcomes. Be gentle with yourself... and others.

Any similarity to the people in this story is simply coincidental. Thank you, celebrities, for being who you are, even though you weren't there.

Becoming a grandmother is wonderful. In one moment you're a mother. The next you are all-wise and prehistoric.
—Pam Brown

To become a grandparent is to enjoy one of the few pleasures in life for which the consequences have already been paid.
—Robert Brault

Grandmother-grandchild relationships are simple. Grandmas are short on criticism and long on love.
—Author Unknown

Researching quotes for my story on grandparenthood was a delight. I could fill pages of the many quotes I loved. I've added the following quotes, as I found them hilarious.

My grandmother started walking five miles a day when she was sixty. She's ninety-seven now, and we don't know where the hell she is.
—Ellen DeGeneres

Grandchildren: the only people who can get more out of you than the IRS.
—Gene Perret

THE JOY OF BEING A GRANDPARENT

ON JUNE 24TH, 1988, one of the greatest gifts of life was bestowed upon my husband and me: the birth of our first grandchild.

I had been working at my desk in Manhattan that morning and jumped into a shower around 12:30 p.m., preparing to meet a friend for lunch. The phone rang. Slathered with soap, I opened the shower door and reached for the phone, which I had placed on the toilet next to the shower. I heard my son, Cliff, ecstatically pronouncing, "Nancy's in labor!"

I rinsed off quickly, called my husband, David, and we arrived at the airport an hour and a half later, to board a 3:30 flight to Denver, Colorado. Alison Rachel Pearl was born a few hours earlier.

My firstborn child now became a father. Where did the years go? Having married at the age of thirty, I knew Cliff was more than ready to be a father. He had always enjoyed being with children. As a high school senior in

Florida, he assumed the role as head of "Big Brothers," and spent many days taking underprivileged children to the beach and other activities. Now he had his own. I knew he'd make a great Dad.

Clifford, my firstborn . . . one month old

The joy on the face of my son, holding his firstborn, was reflected in my own joy. I believe that the joy a grandparent experiences is more than the birth of the next generation, but is the delight in watching your child react to his/her own child. You hope that the love you gave and the lessons you taught in rearing your children will guide your children in raising their own. Parenting is the toughest job there is. There are no courses on how to be a good parent, no universities to offer you a degree in parenthood.

Ali and Daddy, six weeks old

David and I flew to Denver every six weeks from New York City; we couldn't get enough of Alison. Then it became every two months, as the travelling began to wear us down.

I created a special game for Ali; she thought I was a magician or perhaps a *witch*. I collected small samples of lipstick, compacts, keys, and anything I could find that was reduced in size from the norm. I showed her the larger version, then *abracadabra*, I opened my other hand and there was the smaller version. For many years she believed I shrunk the objects. Her big eyes opened wide. "Do it again Grandma." She loved the game, and I did, too!

Each visit to Denver brought us to the Denver Zoo which was Ali's favorite place. Ali loved sitting on Grandpa's shoulders, enjoying the best vantage point of seeing the animals.

Three years later, on June 28th, 1991, Ali's brother, Alex was born. Again, witnessing the ecstatic joy in my son filled my heart to overflowing.

Four days before Alex was born, my younger son, Todd, became a father. When Todd called, late that Monday evening, we hurried to the hospital a few blocks away, and sat in the darkened waiting room of New York University Hospital with his in-laws awaiting the birth. Finally my daughter-in-law, Diane, was wheeled out on a gurney, with an exhausted smile on her face. Joshua Seth Pearl was born . . . our second grandchild. Todd was delirious with joy, having watched his firstborn arrive. Again, my heart was full, not just for myself, but for my son. Todd enjoyed the company of children, especially young children. I've delighted in watching him bring himself down to their level, by immediately sitting on the floor to play with them.

He was always very compassionate. I recall, while in college, a phone call from Todd telling us he missed a major exam. We asked why. He responded, "A friend of mine was in emotional distress and I couldn't leave him alone." Todd missed his calling in life; he should have owned a children's camp. He is totally devoted and committed to fatherhood.

Todd holding Josh, about six weeks old

Two and a half years later, Josh's brother Bradley was born. David and I were now blessed with four grandchildren.

Much has been written about grandparenthood. There are grandparents, out of necessity, that have had to raise their grandchildren; there are those that have been the emotional support for their grandchildren. Then, like so many grandparents, there are those that put a sparkle in the eyes of grandchildren when grandma and grandpa visit.

Dr. Ruth Westheimer says that grandparenting is really just giving your love and your time. "You are not the parent," she argues.

It is true that as grandparents we can enjoy the pleasures without the responsibility of raising them, but the concerns grandparents feel for their grandchildren doesn't differ very much from the concerns that parents feel for their own children.

Living a distance away from our grandchildren made it even more important to share wonderful experiences and fun times with them. Spending many summer weekends together in our Connecticut home with the New York "clan," and the visits from the Colorado family, enjoying boating and fishing on our lake, visiting the Goshen Fair, the birthday parties on the lawn, and playing tennis and golf with them, I believe left my grandchildren with beautiful memories. And me, too!

In the winters at our home in Florida, the visits from the children were also memorable. Staying active with our grandchildren, whenever and wherever we were, enriched our relationship with them, as we were able to maintain an active role in their lives.

When Ali and Alex came to Florida one winter, on school break, Grandpa planned a visit to Disney World. Their Mom and Dad were not interested and decided to visit one of the islands while we had charge of the children. We had an incredible time. The grandchildren went home extolling the trip we shared. The following year, the grandchildren *begged* Grandpa to take them back to Disneyworld again. We received a call from our son asking if we would mind if they joined us, along with our grandchildren. Grandpa hung up the phone and laughed; "It takes children to know what 'good' is." We then proceeded to include a trip on the *Disney Cruise Line,* along with a few days in Disney World. A fabulous time was had by all.

When the grandchildren were young, I loved tucking them into bed at night and telling them stories. Often, I made up stories as I went along. When Bradley was in grade school, I was asked to send some of my stories to school to be read to the class. The children enjoyed my tales, and I hoped it would make Bradley feel special.

When my grandchildren became older, a more adult relationship with them blossomed. I love spending one-on-one dates with them, sharing dinner in a fine restaurant, or going to the theater or an event. Our conversations over dinner are special to me, as I feel their comfort in opening up and talking to me, and that's where the conversation ends . . . only with me. It is so important for your grandchildren to know they can trust you. I also love playing golf with my grandsons, especially when Bradley praises my good shots.

I've often read that grandparents can be "old on the inside but young on the outside." Of the three remaining grandparents, I am the oldest. I often feel like the matriarch of the family. Fortunately, I can still be "young enough" for my grandchildren to enjoy sharing many activities and special time with me.

I lost all of my grandparents before I was ten years old. When my husband, David, passed away, I could relate to the emotional grief of my grandchildren at the loss of their grandfather. Our oldest grandchild, Ali, was thirteen. I was deeply touched that my three younger grandsons wrote and read their own eulogies at their grandpa's funeral.

We had planned an exciting trip abroad for Ali's thirteenth birthday. Unfortunately, Grandpa never made it. Years before, David and I had decided we would take each grandchild, on his/her own, on a special thirteenth birthday trip. When that dream ended, I made a plan of my own.

I decided that I would take the entire family, the ten of us, every five years, on a special trip to celebrate my milestone birthdays. I wanted the grandchildren to share wonderful experiences together. They lived so far apart and had few opportunities to get to know one another; I thought this would be the way to bring the entire family together.

The first family trip was planned. Coming from different parts of the country, we all headed for Hawaii. I was probably more excited than the rest of the family. But still I worried, would everyone get along? To my delight, they did.

The children and grandchildren enjoyed so many exciting activities and adventures together in this beautiful paradise that they had never visited before. My daughter, Tina, presented me with a wonderful gift after I returned home to Florida that fall: a framed picture, prepared like a painting, of our sunset sailing trip off the coast of Oahu.

Five years later, another trip was planned. Our next adventure took us to Bermuda. The most gratifying comment I remember came from my grandson, Bradley. "Can we come back here next year, Grandma?"

My wish is that I can continue this dream of mine . . . these adventures I share with my grandchildren and children. I know my grandchildren will always remember and cherish these special times as they grow older. To

An evening sail with the Pearl family off Oahu

see the delight on their faces has provided me with much happiness. As they say, "What's a grandma for?"

When confronting a difficult situation, my husband, David, often said, "Let's turn a bad thing into a good thing." This attitude often saved the day for many "bad" things.

ON OCTOBER 17TH, 1989, a surface magnitude 7.1 earthquake hit the greater San Francisco and Monterey Bay areas.[1] The devastating earthquake struck at 5:04 p.m., bringing an abrupt halt to the World Series at Candlestick Park in San Francisco.

The Forest of Nisene Marks State Park in Santa Cruz County was the epicenter of the earthquake, which occurred along the San Andreas Fault. The quake was the largest one to erupt along this fault since the "Great San Francisco Earthquake" of 1906.

The 1989 quake became known as Loma Prieta, named after a mountain peak about five miles northeast of the epicenter. It's also been named the World Series Earthquake.

The entire country was informed of the quake—almost immediately— as millions of people were watching television at 5:00 p.m., waiting for the onset of the World Series. Almost every station was announcing the news of the earthquake.

The quake ripped through San Francisco's Marina District causing catastrophic damage. Buildings collapsed and caught on fire, including the home of Joe DiMaggio.

Part of the Cypress Street Viaduct collapsed on the Nimitz Freeway. The upper deck caved in, fell on the lower deck, crushing cars and killing forty-two people.

A section of the upper deck of the San Francisco-Oakland Bay Bridge also gave way and fell on the lower deck.

More than 3,700 people were injured, sixty-seven died and more than twelve thousand were made homeless.

The damage caused by the devastation totaled over $5.9 billion.

Surrounding counties also suffered collapsed buildings, ground ruptures and landslide.

1989: THE SAN FRANCISCO EARTHQUAKE

THE MORNING OF TUESDAY, October 17, 1989, was a cool, but comfortable day in New York City. Heading for the airport, on my way to San Francisco, I wore my usual, comfortable "warm-up" suit for travelling long distances. My husband had flown to Los Angeles over the weekend on business, and was meeting me in San Francisco early that evening.

Our trip would include our annual visit to San Francisco to visit my brother, who lived in Walnut Creek, a small city that lies in the East Bay region of the San Francisco Bay Area.

This year was special, because my brother's son, Steven, had new additions to his family—twin boys, now eight months old. I couldn't wait to see the babies. Steven planned to meet me at the hotel. Then, after lunch, we were going back to his house to see the children.

My plane arrived two hours late, which cancelled lunch. Steven then decided to pick me up at the hotel at 4:00 p.m., and bring me to his house. He suggested that I leave a note in the box for Uncle David, telling him to meet us at his home. I had checked into the Clift Hotel, a favorite of ours, four blocks from Union Square.

When we arrived at Steven's home, a four-story house in the Trocadero area south of San Francisco, I realized it had become very warm.

I was given the *grand tour* of the very interesting house that my niece, Linda, and my nephew, Steven, had re-constructed from one of the older homes. They were both architectural interior designers, and had done a beautiful job.

The master bedroom was on the top floor, with a large terrace outside. One of the twins had awakened from his nap, while the other twin slept down below. Steven carried the baby to the outside terrace, while my niece, Linda, brought cold drinks.

We sat for a short time on the terrace, under the intense sun. It had turned from warm to hot. I asked Steven for a tee shirt, as the sweatshirt I was wearing was very uncomfortable.

Linda placed the drinks on the table and stood next to us, as Steven and I sat, about to lift our glasses. Suddenly, I saw my glass slowly walking across the table. Then I heard Linda scream, "Steven, it's an earthquake! Grab the baby!" It was just past 5:00 p.m.

They both ran down the staircase, while clutching the baby, to the lower level to retrieve the other infant from his crib.

I ran after them, but I couldn't walk down the stairs—everything was shaking violently. I sat on my backside and maneuvered myself down the stairs, one step at a time.

When I reached the bottom of the steps, I saw Steven and Linda lying on the floor in the center of the hallway, next to the dining room. They were lying on top of each twin, protecting them from any falling debris.

They told me you must remain in an open area, not beneath a doorway or low ceiling. I lay down on the floor next to them. When I looked up, I saw silver candlesticks idling across the length of the long, granite dining table. The glass-enclosed artwork on the wall came crashing down, sending pieces of flying glass everywhere.

Then . . . quiet. The shaking had ceased. But, the aftershocks continued sporadically after the original quake.

Within the next hour, friends began arriving at the house. Steven's house was about a mile or so from Candlestick Park. Linda's brother had been at the stadium for the World Series, as had many of their friends. They walked the distance from the stadium to the house, as there was no transportation to get home, since most of them had taken the metro.

Communication was sporadic. My brother, somehow, was able to call us from his side of the bay. He was instructed to call my parents in Florida. They, in turn, called my son in Colorado, who was home, as was my dad, to watch the World Series. My son reached my daughter and she called my other son in New York. The message was: *Mom is okay, and at Steven's home.*

No other calls got through until, miraculously, I received a call from my daughter, Tina. "Dad called, and he was crying on the phone." My husband was a very emotional man. "He boarded the plane in L.A., before 5:00 p.m., and shortly after that they announced that the flight was cancelled, as there had been a major earthquake in San Francisco."

Tina continued the lengthy story. "Again, they announced that they were being rerouted to Sacramento, and anyone who wished to remain on board would need to travel to San Francisco by other means. Dad said he was continuing on board to Sacramento."

My husband told me later that when he arrived in Sacramento, he quickly exited the plane, ran to the first car-rental counter and was lucky to rent the last available car. Then he called Tina to tell her that he was coming to get me, and would keep in touch with her.

Fortunately, I heard from Tina again. When she gave me her father's message, I told her, when her father called, to tell him, "He cannot come into San Francisco."

The gentleman sitting next to my husband aboard the plane was next in line at the car-rental, but none were left. He asked my husband if he could share the expense of the rental and be dropped off at his home on the way into San Francisco. My husband graciously offered to take him home, without any expense, as he had enjoyed the man's company on the trip to Sacramento. The gentleman was a senior executive of one of the largest oil companies in the United States.

When they arrived at his home, close to 12:30 a.m., the man's wife insisted that my husband remain with them overnight, telling my husband that the authorities were not allowing anyone into the city at that time.

About 1:00 a.m., I received a phone call from my husband. Again, I don't know how he got through, as communications were at a standstill.

I was sleeping on the sofa in my nephew's den, as friends were sleeping on the floor in every room. As I spoke to my husband, I was thrown off the sofa from another major aftershock.

Happy that I was safe, my husband planned to drive into the city the following day and meet me at the hotel.

The morning arrived and all was quiet. Steven drove me back to the Clift Hotel about 10:30 a.m. The city looked like a ghost town; it was a heartbreaking sight.

I was in shock when I arrived at the hotel. I had the sense that this was not real. This was a movie being filmed and I was playing a role. The lobby was a scene from a war-torn film. The woman behind the front desk appeared as if she had been there through the night. Her clothes were disheveled and she was covered in dust. Her hair hung in disarray. The note I had left in the box for my husband was still in the small cubicle behind her.

There was debris everywhere. Columns were cracked and the elevators were dead. I was on the tenth floor so I took the back staircase to reach my room. But, it was difficult to climb the stairs, as many people were walking down, carrying their heavy suitcases. They reminded me of immigrants fleeing a war.

I looked up into the open stairwell to the floors above and noticed a deep crack in the surrounding wall, which ran all the way to the top. I prayed, as I slowly climbed, that the ceiling would not give way.

When I reached my room and opened the door, I could not believe what I saw. There was the destruction of the lobby and everywhere I turned but my room was just as I had left it: untouched by the ravages of the earthquake.

I quickly re-packed my suitcase, carried it down the ten flights of stairs, and checked my bag with the concierge. I then went outside to the street to await my husband.

Within twenty minutes, I saw him about two blocks away. When he saw me, we both began running toward each other. As we reached each other, he lifted me up into the air, kissing me and turning in circles. This was *definitely* a scene from a movie. I could even hear the music.

We spotted a phone booth, leaning on an angle. My husband reached for the phone while I placed my back against the booth, again, praying it wouldn't collapse. I did a lot of praying that day. Luckily, the phone worked.

With a smile on his face, he emerged from the phone booth and said, "I just called Auberge du Soleil. We are driving to Napa Valley for lunch, and they may, possibly, have a room for us for the night, as they were receiving cancellations."

When we arrived they were delighted to tell us that one of their magnificent suites had just become available, and we could have it for two days.

After relaxing and enjoying the beautiful scenery, the wonderful food and the romantic interlude with the man I loved, we met my brother and his wife for a three-day trip back to Sacramento. We stayed at a charming country inn. The remainder of our trip was a delight.

We had pursued our original plan to spend this time with my brother, and I also had been able to see my nephew's twins . . . if only for a short time.

When we finally returned home to New York City, I thought, *He did it again.* My husband often had a way of turning something bad into something good.

Don't be sorry about the things you haven't accomplished. If the desire still exists and the opportunity arises… DO IT! And pat yourself on the back. It is never too late to create something new.

FIRST TIME PUBLISHED: A WINNER

WHEN I RETURNED FROM CHAUTAUQUA one summer, after a second year of an invigorating, exciting week of lectures, lessons and inspiring advice at the ninth annual Highlights Conference, I decided to write a story that had been fermenting in my head for more than a year. Like fine wine, it was ready to be poured.

The story was about an interracial relationship. My intention was to write it for a specific magazine. The protagonist was older than most of the characters in my short stories and I decided it had to be told in the first person. Everything seemed to be out of my normal realm of writing. I usually wrote stories for younger children, and rarely wrote in first person. This story would be a first for me in many ways.

Although I had been writing for almost four years, and had received encouragement and praise from both professionals and friends, discouragement was beginning to take hold. I had never been published.

I checked my *Writer's Market* to see if the magazine where I wanted to submit my story was still in publication. It was. Then I remembered that this magazine had an annual short story contest. Why not write the story for the contest? Nothing to lose. Great!

I discovered the deadline for the contest was eight days away, and I wasn't able to start until two days later. The pressure was on; it became my fuel. What a challenge! Was I capable of writing a story of over two thousand words, with revisions, etc., for a YA and adult magazine—in such a short span of time? I was determined to try.

At 7:30 a.m., I sat down at my computer and remained there for thirteen hours. The following day, I returned to the computer for a final twelve hours. I immersed myself in the role of the young girl with a passion. I became a one-woman show—playing all the characters—laughing and talking to myself, as my fingers tapped out my feelings. This was the longest, most emotionally involved, mature story I had ever attempted to write. And it began without a title or characters names, and only a few scribbled notes. The idea alone existed in my mind. Twenty-five hours later my story was revised, polished and ready to go.

I made the deadline. I called the magazine to let them know I had sent my story Federal Express as time was too short for regular mail. I was surprised when it was the editor who answered the phone. She had received my story and had just finished reading it.

"I love your story. I cried," she said. "This is a true story, isn't it?"

After catching my breath, I assured her that bits and pieces of the story were taken from real life, but, the story was fiction. She said she couldn't promise that I would win the contest; there were so many good stories—but she wanted to publish it. I hung up the phone and screamed!

That September, my story was published. It won second place in the annual short story contest sponsored by *Aim Magazine*. My first published story . . . a contest winner! What a thrill!

I found myself jumping into the roles of all my characters after that, whether they were frogs or bunnies, boys or girls. Did I have to push myself again, with limited time, to write a good story? I hoped not. I was emotionally drained. But I did learn a very good lesson: Immerse yourself in the character and LET GO. What comes out could very well be a winner.

My story, "A-1 Granny Sitting Service," won second place among five winners; it was published by *Aim Magazine*.

A favorite affirmation of Charles Fillmore was, "Faith is the strength of the soul inside, and lost is the man without it."

1995: THE YEAR OF THE MIRACLE

I'VE ALWAYS BELIEVED THAT God tests us. He pushes us to our outer limits and if our faith and strength remain intact, he rewards us—sometimes with a miracle. 1995 was just such a year.

In the summer of 1992, my husband and I bought property on a beautiful lake in Connecticut and hired an architect to design our dream house. My husband, David, was planning to retire within the next few years, and we wanted this house to be really special. All our energies went into the planning and execution of this major undertaking, for the house doubled in size as we kept finding new ideas and additions. Friends and relatives teased us about people getting divorced over building a house like this. We had *no clue* it would take almost three years to complete, and within those three years we would be faced with heart-breaking family issues. God was working over-time.

David's mother was diagnosed with ovarian cancer. I moved my parents from Florida to Stamford, Connecticut and back to Florida as my Dad was not well. In January, 1994 he passed away, and my mother had a breakdown. I then moved my mother back north to watch over her. When those three years were over, we breathed a great sigh of relief.

Our weekend house in Connecticut was slow in selling and finally, after one year, a delightful couple bought it. We planned our move into the new house the first week of May, 1995.

As January of 1995, arrived, my mother-in-law took a turn for the worse. By mid-March she was critical, and my husband spent most of the month with her. I remained up north packing up the old house. On March 29th, she died. Soon after, we left for Connecticut to continue the burdensome job of packing and cleaning out the garage and basement of the old house. We felt we had been pushed to our limit—but God wasn't finished.

On Sunday, April 9th, Bob and Monique, the couple that bought our house, came to visit with a tape measure. My husband excused himself to attend to some work in the garage. Shortly after, Bob and Monique left.

Minutes later, the doorbell rang. "Call 911," Bob yelled. "David had an accident and he can't move!"

I numbly reached for the phone and dialed 911 without fully absorbing what Bob had said, then ran out of the house towards the garage. David was lying on the cold, cement floor of the garage, paralyzed. A gravity exercise machine, stored in the garage, had flipped him on his head as he leaned on it, and was now lying at his feet. He looked up at me with tears in his eyes and kept repeating, "I'm sorry, honey, I'm so sorry."

The ambulance soon arrived and the EMTs took over. They were very professional and handled David with great care, gently placing his neck in two halves of a neck brace, and strapping him to a board which they slid under his body to keep him immobilized. By this time, he was able to wiggle his fingers and toes, slightly.

When we arrived at the emergency room of our small country hospital, tests and x-rays were ordered immediately. The unthinkable had happened! David had broken his neck.

David was in agony, but the doctor was only able to give him a small shot to relieve pain, as the drug could nauseate him. He could possibly regurgitate lying on his back and would choke. It was imperative that he remain still.

"Please, honey, don't let anyone touch me but Steven," David pleaded. "Promise me."

Steven was a brilliant spinal surgeon and the stepson of David's sister, but here we were in northern Connecticut and Steven's hospital was in Morristown, New Jersey. I promised him I would honor his request.

It was late Sunday afternoon when I called my sister-in-law and got the number of Steven's country club. He was having an early dinner with his family. He was a tower of strength for me, handling matters with the doctor in the emergency room. "Keep him overnight, as I don't like moving my spinal cord injuries at night," said Steven. But they couldn't keep David, as there was no neurology department at the hospital, and therefore, no neurologist. They wanted to airlift him to Hartford Hospital. "No," Steven said, "airlift him to Morristown Memorial instead."

The emergency room doctor made arrangements for David to be airlifted to New Jersey, but two hours later the pilot called back informing us that a major storm was going to hit the Northeast within the next hour or two. The flight was cancelled.

We had no choice. After conferring with Steven, the doctor made arrangements for a private ambulance. At 9:00 p.m., after five hours in the emergency room, we departed for a three-and-a-half hour journey, through a nor'easter, on our way to Morristown Memorial Hospital, a world-renowned trauma center in New Jersey.

When we arrived, at 12:30 a.m., Steven was waiting.

As he whisked David away, I saw my son Todd walking through the door. Twenty minutes later, my daughter, Tina, and her friend Monica arrived. They had all travelled a long distance in the storm. I knew I had to be strong and give them a sense of hope. I told them Dad was in wonderful hands and Steven would do everything in his power to make Dad well.

I watched as Steven drilled holes on either side of David's head and placed screws to hold the halo with weights on it to align the broken vertebrae in his neck. He had the worst break—between the first and second vertebrae. At 2:00 a.m., Steven told us David was stabilized. "Go home," he said. "I want him to remain like this for another day. I'll operate Tuesday morning."

I held each of my children as they sobbed in my arms. I kept telling myself, "Stay strong, Mona, stay strong."

David remained in intensive care with the halo and its weights doing their job. The realignment of the vertebrae would be ready for surgery Tuesday morning, just as Steven had planned. Monday night, I begged Steven to be honest with me. I had to prepare myself for the worst. He rattled off percentages about dying on the table or being paralyzed for life. I didn't like the odds. But, then he put his arms around me and said, "Don't worry, I've done this surgery many times before and I know I can do it. He's going to be okay." At that moment, I was unaware that Steven had an internal struggle over whether to operate on a close family relative, but, as he told his wife, "I can do it better than anyone else."

At 6:00 a.m., the following morning I arrived at the hospital. I went to the phone and called Silent Unity in Missouri. A gentle voice answered, asking how she could help. I told her about David and asked her to pray for him. She spoke to me for a while, then assured me they would pray for David around the clock for thirty days. I hung up the phone with a sense of peace, knowing that the surgery was going to be successful. David was going to be okay.

I had not called my older son, Clifford, living in Colorado, as he and his wife had left for Mexico the day before for a much-needed rest. Now, I had to tell them. I reassured them that they did not have to fly home, that Dad was going to make it, and I would keep them informed. They agreed to remain in Mexico; I promised I would tell them the truth.

Tuesday morning, I sat in the recovery waiting room, during the surgery, with Todd, Tina and Monica. We read, chatted and even joked about earlier times in their childhood. After four and a half hours, Steven and his associate, Carl, came into the waiting room. The surgery was over. I looked at Steven's smiling face and knew he had kept his promise. David was going to be well again . . . and he was. One week later, he walked away from the hospital.

David struggled through months of pain and discomfort and rarely complained. He couldn't sleep, because the collar he wore made it impossible, so he wandered the apartment at night. He could barely eat, because it was difficult to chew and the food dribbled into the collar. But, as time passed he became stronger, and finally he was able to discard the collar. On his x-rays he looked like the robotic man, wired up with titanium, but he was perfectly normal.

After a full recovery, he walked, talked, exercised, golfed, drove, danced, worked on his computer and loved with a heart bigger than ever. When I looked at him, I truly knew what faith and miracles were all about.

In May, 1995, five weeks after David's accident, Christopher Reeve broke his neck. The injury to the vertebrae was almost identical; the results, as the world knows, were tragically different.

Do you see how the god always hurls his bolts at the greatest houses and the tallest trees. For he is wont to thwart whatever is greater than the rest.
　—Herodotus

The more enlightened our houses are, the more their walls ooze ghosts.
　—Italo Calvino

They say that shadows of deceased ghosts
Do haunt the houses and the graves about,
Of such whose life's lamp went untimely out,
Delighting still in their forsaken hosts.
　—Joshua Sylvester

Researching quotes on houses, I found many which "spoke" to me. All of the above seemed to have touched my soul. I believe there is a story behind every door.

THE HOUSE

STANDING PROUDLY HIGH ABOVE the lake, three stories high and 120 feet long, the house retained its own personality. The hill, dressed in a magnificent array of flowers in a multitude of colors, began at the rear of the house and sloped steeply downward towards the edge of the lake. In the eight years I lived in this incredible structure, I came to realize it had a life of its own.

The first photo was taken in the fall of 1994, six months before moving into the house. The hill had not yet been planted, but within a year it was so breathtaking that it was included in the *White Flower Farm Catalog,* mailed throughout the country. (2nd photo)

The property we purchased was heavily wooded and had the old, low stone walls running throughout. Within the previous century, much of Connecticut property was defined and divided by these low stone walls. There were no remnants left of the houses or barns or any other structures, but stories circulated about former owners of some of the properties in the area. Was there a story attached to the property we bought? Were there possibly graves hidden in the confines of the woods? I'll never know, but over the years I've come to believe there may have been.

We hired a brilliant, young architect who designed a one-of-a-kind house that reached 4,500 square feet when he presented the final plans. But final . . . it was not.

After visiting our son, Cliff, in Colorado, where Cliff took us to see some showcase houses, we returned to Connecticut with more ideas and changed the original plans three times. The house evolved into just under 10,000 square feet. I often joked that the house became pregnant.

The excavation for the house began in 1992, and then a steel frame of the structure was erected. The committee at our lake community informed us that we were not permitted to build any commercial buildings on the lake. They thought we were erecting a small hotel.

Our plan was to retire in our "dream house." We built an elevator shaft to house an eventual elevator installed when we grew older, if we needed it. We had a home theater, a playroom for the grandchildren, a playroom for the "big boys" with a pool table, a sauna, a library and guest rooms for family and friends on the third floor. A glass atrium ran from the ground to the third floor with beautiful views of the lake from almost every room in the house.

There were five fireplaces (two were double-sided), and the master suite had steps leading down to our private office. The house was incredible. It was photographed for an ad in *Architectural Digest,* and was on the cover of a new "home" magazine. We couldn't wait to move in.

One month before our moving date, in May, 1995, my husband, David, had his tragic accident. He had broken his neck and could not be moved. He remained in our apartment in New York City, while I moved into the house alone. This was not the welcome I expected from a house that we had poured our hearts and souls into.

A month after the move, I was able to bring David to his new house. He was ecstatic, as David was a Pisces, and loved the water. He would sit on the deck each morning, enjoying the view of our five-mile-perimeter lake. We bought a pontoon boat, large enough for family and friends to enjoy a jaunt on the lake, and left it moored at our dock.

Many evenings, as I was preparing dinner, David would take the boat out by himself. He would say, "I'm taking a short run to 'blow off the stink.'" This was his greatest stress reducer. The lake was potable and clear as crystal. The children and grandchildren swam in the lake and fished off the dock. My grandson, Joshua, kept a chart of how many fish he caught and hung it in the garage above the rack that held their fishing rods. I recall the last count at twenty-three. Grandpa insisted on catch and release.

My sons, Cliff and Todd, and my three little fishermen and one fisherwoman.

We had memorable birthday parties on the lawn overlooking the lake. Three of my four grandchildren had their birthdays the same week in June— two on the same day. My grandson, Brad, the youngest, was the only December child. He was allowed to share the birthday celebration with his "half-birthday." His name was always included, along with the other three, on the birthday cake.

Both photos are of only one of my two English flower gardens, in which I indulged my love of flower arranging. At least twice a week I gathered flowers, filling vases throughout the house with brilliant color and sweet fragrances, bringing the outdoors in.

The summers and the early fall were glorious. Mother Nature's most talented artists painted their beautiful landscape surrounding the lake, which reflected in the water like a mirror when autumn arrived.

Autumn on the lake

We remained in the house that first winter while David was recovering from his accident. The snow, trickling down softly, created a fairyland effect upon the lake. Canadian geese came ashore at the edge of the lake, spread their wings and lay on their backs, whenever the sun peeked through.

The deer, foraging for food, came visiting almost every morning, and wild turkeys marched in a column with their young, searching for edibles in the frozen ground. Even red fox decided this was the place to find a treat here and there.

The area of Connecticut where we built our house was in the northwest corner of the state in the foothills of the Berkshires. There was so much to keep one involved and well fed. The Goshen Fair was ten minutes up the road, and also offered jazz concerts in the summer. Wonderful restaurants were abundant within a half hour away. We joined a golf club ten minutes from home. There was skiing, sledding and ice-skating in the winter. Summer stock afforded entertainment within an hour from the house and Tanglewood, the famous outdoor concert venue for the Boston Pops, was also an hour away.

The children loved visiting and especially enjoyed early evening jaunts on the boat before dinner. We drank champagne and feasted on hors d'oeuvres as we sailed on the private lake. This was paradise . . . everything David and I had planned for the future in our "dream house."

Within a year after we moved into the house, we went to California to visit my brother, Mike, who had undergone brain surgery for Parkinson's disease. The morning we were returning to Connecticut, we received a phone call from Jimmy, the man who worked for us and took care of the property. Our house sat many feet below the main road above. There had been a break in the sewage pipes and the entire lower level of our house was flooded with sewage.

We returned to a horrendous mess. Sewage was in the air-conditioning ducts and had destroyed the carpets, some of the furniture, clothes hanging in the lower level cedar closets and much more. The house had not yet celebrated its first anniversary.

We brought in an excellent company that ozonated, fumigated, aerated, *everythingated* the house to make it livable again. We remained in our apartment in New York City for about a month until our house welcomed our return.

After the third winter, spent in Florida, we returned to Connecticut in the spring of 1998, and discovered the roof tiles were cracking and falling to the ground. We had fallen in love with a tile roof we had seen in Colorado many years before. The tile appeared to be green slate, but was faux. Unbeknownst to us, the government had imposed new regulations on the company that produced the tile. It removed the asbestos from the product and it weakened the integrity of the tile. With the extreme changes in temperature from winter to summer, the tile began to disintegrate. We found pieces of broken tile everywhere. We had no choice but to replace a 120-foot-long roof with new indestructible shingles.

Life continued as the seasons came and went. Was our house speaking to us? We wished it well.

Within another two years, the window frames, made of wood, began rotting and leaking. Again, unbeknownst to us, the company that produced the windows went out of business, as they had major problems with their windows. We needed to replace about 120 windows and some doors. At this point, David was ready to give up. We talked about selling the house even though we had loved our house with a passion and had many beautiful memories in spite of the problems.

We decided to replace all the windows, enjoy the house for another year or two after that, then buy a condo on a golf course in Connecticut. David was tired of all the responsibility and the problems. After three major episodes in five years, he was ready to throw in the proverbial towel. We became fearful of leaving our house each winter. It seemed like the house was upset and angry when we left it alone and wanted to punish us when we returned.

In the spring of 2001, when we returned to Connecticut, David was already ill with lung cancer. The windows were still being replaced. He never saw the completed job.

After David passed away in September, 2001, I continued to live alone in the house for another two years. Checking to ensure that the eleven entries to the house were locked each night, I amazingly slept soundly. I was concerned that I would feel frightened and uncomfortable living in the house alone. The house became quiet and peaceful, as if it had purged itself from its bad behavior. It seemed to envelop me in its womb and watched over me as a parent watches over its child. I felt safe. Yet, I sensed there was a story that lived on the property of my beloved house.

Or could it have been David watching over me? After David's burial, that afternoon, Tina was walking down the long hallway to my bedroom. As she passed the archway leading into the living room, she saw the shadow of a man standing near the sofa at the end of the room. She entered the living room and sat down on the sofa. She later revealed to me that Dad had visited her and gave her a message for me. The message was, "Tell Mom not to sell the house." David knew I loved the house and wasn't happy about the idea of selling it.

A year after David passed away, Jimmy was outside cleaning the large stone table, which sat in front of the atrium. He had the strange feeling he was being watched. He looked up and saw David standing on the third level of the tall, glass atrium, watching him. He was visibly shaken. He told his wife what had happened, but was unable to tell me about the incident until the following year.

In June, 2003, I sold the house. Having moved into the house alone in 1995, I moved out alone in October, 2003.

The couple that bought my house was very enthusiastic about their purchase. They were of Chinese heritage and continued the custom of naming their home. The wife wanted to name the house I loved the "Jade House." Her husband said no. He named the house the "Pearl House" in honor of my deceased husband.

The stone table where Jimmy looked up to see
David standing on the third level of the glass atrium

Part Three

THE TRAVELLING YEARS

With David: 1980s & 1990s

Travelling became an integral part of our lives when we realized the importance of getting away alone. For thirty-one years David and I roamed the world, laughing and loving along the way.

A dear friend of David's, an older gentleman, once told David the secret to keeping romance alive. "Treat your wife like a mistress. Take her out each week . . . alone. Wine her and dine her and make love often. That's what keeps romance alive." We heeded his advice.

Every Wednesday, I kissed my children goodbye, took the Long Island Railroad into New York City to meet David for dinner. We often pretended we were on a date, and did a lot of flirting.

Our travels were like extended dates. I believe his friend's advice was the glue that kept the romance intact. Travelling afforded the freedom from work and the responsible but rewarding job of raising a family.

The following stories of our travels are stories of our love and romance that survived forty-six years.

See the world through different eyes. Take from other lands that which you can use to enrich your life, and hopefully, give back to others that which can enrich theirs.

WANDERLUST II: 1980-1982

1980: WHERE DID THE TIME GO? It seemed we had just returned from our twentieth anniversary trip a short time ago, and now we were off on another adventure to celebrate our twenty-fifth anniversary. Our wanderlust was nipping at our heels.

We decided on a cruise, since we found it to be so relaxing without having to pack and unpack and race to an airport. Our sons were working and Tina was away at camp for the summer. All of this contributed to a very relaxed and romantic vacation.

We flew into Milan and took a delightful day trip into Switzerland. We ascended the high cliff above Lake Lugano; the view of the lake from the top of the cliff was spectacular, then afterwards we drove to San Bernardino.

Overlooking Lake Lugano: July, 1980

Two days later, we boarded our ship, the *Sagafjord*, leaving from Genoa. Travelling south along the west coast of Italy, through the Tyrrhenian Sea, we stopped at the Isle of Capri. We took the funicular to reach the town of Capri, which rests high above the harbor. Capri is an enchanting place, deserving of the songs that have been written about it. David spotted a jewelry store with the name Perla, and said we had to buy a memento from a store that carried our name in Italian. Lucky me! He bought me a ring, which I continued to wear as a wedding ring for the rest of my married life.

We continued on, past the "Boot of Italy" into the Ionian Sea to reach Athens. Having visited Athens a few years earlier, we instead took advantage of resting aboard the ship.

In the evenings, David and I enjoyed our favorite exercise: dancing. David was a great dancer; he had his father's genes. My father-in-law danced in competition against George Raft, the famous movie actor. My father-in-law won. But dancing with David was a sensually romantic experience. People often asked if we were professional and sometimes cleared the floor to watch us dance.

The food on the ship was *scrumptious*; we ate ourselves into oblivion. It seemed like every few hours buffets were being offered, with great presentations. I learned a great lesson while dining aboard a cruise ship. Never go to the midnight buffet, eat a hearty breakfast, a salad for lunch and no dessert for dinner. You can nibble a small treat mid-afternoon but pace yourself or you may need to be lifted off the ship by a crane.

Oh my God . . . forget dieting!

The ship left Athens through the Aegean Sea and travelled through the Dardanelles Strait into the Black Sea. I was looking forward to arriving in Russia, as our first port was Odessa, the place of my grandmother's birth. I tried to find information about my grandmother's family to no avail. The next port was Yalta, where the famous Yalta Conference was held.

We loved cruising and planned to take advantage of this wonderful way to travel. We thought of living on bread and water for the week after we returned home, but the thought only remained a thought. The few extra pounds were worth it!

1981: We went to Mexico City to visit a friend living there. We had never been to Mexico, other than a day trip to Tijuana, crossing the border while staying in San Diego.

We took a day trip to visit the remains of the Great Temple of Tenochtitlan, and the pyramid of Tenayuca. Having been to Egypt in 1975, we were astounded by the similarity. We climbed to the top. David's opinion was that the continents were connected long ago and people travelled across the continents bringing their culture and traditions with them. Researchers and scientists agree with this theory, as we discovered later.

The highlight of the trip was the dinner, given in our honor, at the home of our friends. The guests were Spanish/English-speaking and were among the elite of Mexico. Our host had a prominent position in Mexican society, but lived quietly behind high stone walls, and spoke only Spanish. Our hostess spoke perfect English. David was fluent in Spanish and chatted with our host and the other guests. I just smiled, pretending to enjoy the conversations, as I didn't understand a word. Occasionally, they realized I didn't speak the language and would speak in English for a few moments. The dinner was very formal, with butlers standing behind us ready to serve our every need.

David loved being able to converse in Spanish; he spoke like a native. On the way back to our hotel in the taxi, he whispered some Spanish words in my ear. Although I didn't understand the language, there are some words in every language that don't need interpretation.

Another evening, our friends took us to dinner in a park in the middle of the city. Driving there our hostess missed the entrance to the park where the restaurant was. David suggested we stop to ask the police, who were sitting in their car close by.

"Oh! No!" she replied. "You never stop to ask anything of the police. It's quite dangerous."

We were shocked and quite disturbed over her reply. We had heard stories about the police in those years, but didn't believe them. I hope today the story is different.

We said our farewells to our friends and went to Acapulco for a few days, enjoying long walks on the beautiful beach, which ran for miles.

When we returned home we realized how much there was to see and enjoy on this side of the Atlantic. We loved travelling abroad, with its ancient history, but there is so much history in our own country, on our own continent. We had been to Canada, many places in the United States, and now Mexico, but we had never visited South America. Perhaps, some day in the future, I will visit my sister continent.

1982: In the early 1980s, David became a member of the board of a mental health clinic. The members often travelled to exotic places. When they asked us to join them on a trip to China, we jumped at the opportunity. It was a small group of twenty, and we would be travelling with our own guide throughout China. I wasn't too excited about the prospect of travelling with a group of psychiatrists. I hoped I wouldn't be analyzed along the way.

We headed for the Orient on a cool day in April, stopping to change planes in Los Angeles, before the fifteen-hour flight to Hong Kong.

Arriving in Hong Kong in the early morning, we could view some of Hong Kong's 235 islands through the aircraft window. Viewing Hong Kong Harbor was an impressive experience, as the city was massive.

Hong Kong Harbor—early-morning aerial view (two photos used to create panorama)

The people wore the traditional dress, and seemed to spend their lives on the bustling streets. We spent a fascinating day visiting Aberdeen, with its world-famous floating restaurants and hundreds of junks and sampans, where over twenty thousand people live on the water. Looking back from today's perspective, I am so glad that David and I were able to visit China before it became as modernized as it is today. At the time, we felt it hadn't changed in a thousand years. Friends who have travelled to China in recent years tell me I wouldn't recognize it.

We tried to explore every corner of Hong Kong in the time we had, as we were leaving for Mainland China in a few days. We began our adventure into China in Guangzhou (Canton), the southern gateway to China. One could take a hydrofoil from Hong Kong to Canton.

Two days later, we boarded a plane to Guilin (Kweilin), one of China's most famous, scenic cities, only forty minutes by air from Canton.

We were told to pack one medium suitcase per person, as the planes and buses could not accommodate too much luggage. I wore black almost every day, so it never showed any soil.

Our hotel was along a river, and each morning we watched an interesting scene. Men, women and children would come down to the river for their daily routines. One woman knelt at the edge of the river washing clothes. Another woman was bathing her young child; a man emptied a pail of refuse into the river. On the other side of the river, two young men were using the river for a toilet. It was shocking to us, but this was their way of life.

Guilin is world-famous for its extraordinary scenery. The landscape looks like a traditional Chinese painting in ink and color. Guilin is a city of lofty, weird shaped pinnacles, hills and caverns, thrust up by the crustal movements of the earth. The shapes created names for many of the hills like Elephant Trunk Hill, Camel Hill and Old Man Hill. Early morning presents an eerie scene with the rising mist among the craggy shapes.

The morning mist rising over the craggy hills of Guilin

We took a six-hour boat ride south from Guilin on the Lijiang River (Li River), which runs past the city. The sights along the way seemed almost unreal. We stopped at what appeared to be an ancient village. A little old man, who also appeared ancient, went about his chores along the river.

When we boarded the boat, my husband noticed a large monkey or chimpanzee in a cage sitting on the deck. "It looks like we'll have entertainment on board," David said.

After a fascinating six hours and a tasty lunch that appeared to be pork, we returned to shore. The cage was empty. David asked the captain where the monkey was. The answer: "Lunch."

We left for Shanghai the following morning. Shanghai, with its population of about eleven million people, is one of the world's largest cities.

In 1982, the air in Shanghai, I believe, was cleaner than it is today. There were few cars on the road, but hundreds of bicycles converged from every direction. One had to be careful when walking, as the bicyclists often didn't stop. This was true of most of the cities we visited in China.

One evening we went to a nightclub. We felt as if we were back in time during World War II. There were young Chinese men in uniform dancing with their girlfriends to the tunes from the early 40s. They went from dancing a slow trot to the jitterbug. David and I joined the dancing and the dancers on the floor loved our dance routines and asked us to show them a few steps. We did and then they applauded us. It was great fun!

The people were very friendly and seemed quite happy to have Americans visiting their country. One young man came up to us on the street, bowed and asked if he might speak to us. He wanted to practice his English. When we told him he spoke quite well, he smiled and bowed again, thanking us profusely. We asked him where he learned to speak English. He answered, "Watch television. Follow the bouncing ball. Ball follows English sentence. Learn very quickly."

Our next city was Xian, one of the six ancient cities of China. The most famous site, which draws tourists from all over the world, is the Tomb of Qin Shi Huang Di, known as the Tomb of the Clay Warriors. This mausoleum is more than two thousand years old.

There were a thousand life-size, terra cotta warriors and horses guarding the main entrance of the tomb of the Qin emperor. In 1974, the tomb was accidently discovered by a group of local peasants who were digging an irrigation well. This remains as one of the most impressive archeological sites I have seen in my lifetime.

David held his camera, dangling along his leg, and kept snapping pictures below us of the tomb while nonchalantly looking the other way. I almost screamed, "David, they're going to arrest us. We're going to end up in a Chinese jail!" The sign said, STRICTLY NO PHOTOGRAPHS.

Warriors and horses from the Tomb of the Clay Warriors

121

Beijing (Peking), China's capital, was the last city on this extraordinary visit to China, before we left this great empire. There was so much to see in this historic and captivating city. The names of Kublai Khan and Marco Polo resonated there.

We visited the Forbidden City, which housed the Imperial Palace complex. The gardens were beautiful, especially the cascading wisteria. Three weeks after we returned home David was watching a TV movie. "Mona," he screamed, "come in here. The Forbidden City is in the movie. We just walked through the same rooms."

The Garden of the Imperial Palace

Wisteria in the garden of the Imperial Palace

Tiananmen Square, the largest public square in the world, is surrounded by many important monuments and buildings, including the Mao Zedong Memorial Hall.

We toured Mao's mausoleum in the Memorial building where his tomb is located. His preserved body is on display for visitors to view. There is also a wax model of his body, so real that you think you are viewing the actual body. We never knew if we actually saw the real Mao or the wax figure.

Relaxing on an elephant in Beijing

Two days before we left China, we went for the long journey on the Great Wall. It was a cool, overcast day, which made it easier for the up-hill trek. I don't remember how many miles we walked . . . probably no more than two, but it seemed much longer.

A segment of the Great Wall

Another segment of the Great Wall

The Great Wall was built over two thousand years ago. The peasants worked on the wall for 1,700 years; it extends about 5,500 miles. Our guide told us that many people lived and died on the wall, and never left it, while it was being built. The wall was originally designed to keep the Mongol nomads out of China. It wasn't successful. We were so fascinated by the history of the wall, and remained staring out from the wall, imagining the Mongols riding their horses towards China preparing to invade the country.

Our last night in Beijing we enjoyed a wonderful banquet. I had the best Peking duck I have ever eaten in my life.

We left our group of twenty, and continued on our own to Japan. But, unfortunately, our visit to Japan was cut short after three days. I developed dysentery after leaving China and could barely digest water. I struggled to enjoy what I could, knowing we would probably not return to Japan for many years.

We took a day trip to Nikko on the "bullet train," and we visited a Japanese shrine and watched the red-robed monks at their daily prayers. We returned to the States the next day. Happily though, I wasn't diagnosed along the way. The psychiatrists were on vacation and had left their psychiatric skills at home.

I have always wanted to return to Japan. Sadly, with the enormous devastation Japan endured in 2011, I doubt I will be able to fulfill this dream. My prayers are with the people of Japan.

Travelling can become an addiction. The more you see, the more you want to see. The world is a fascinating place.

CRUISE MANIA

THE CRUISE BUG REALLY bit the both of us. Having loved the Black Sea cruise in 1980, we decided to take the Baltic Sea cruise in 1983 on the *Vistafjord*, the sister ship to the *Sagafjord*.

Before sailing out of Hamburg, we took a side trip to Amsterdam. The canals contribute to making Amsterdam a very picturesque place.

A canal in Amsterdam

While visiting the city we went to the Anne Frank House. I climbed the narrow stairs to the attic where she kept her diary that later was published as *The Diary of a Young Girl.* I could almost feel the emotions of this young girl, while hiding with her family from the Nazis, living at the top of the house that was part of her father's office building. The family was finally betrayed and was transported to concentration camps.

David was so overcome by the experience that he went down to the street, with tears in his eyes, to breathe fresh air, while I continued the tour on my own. I have found that the emotions of passionate men like David often erupted into tears when confronted with heart-wrenching and even heart-warming situations. David frequently became tearful in sad movies. *I love a man who cries.* Returning to Hamburg, we boarded the *Vistafjord* on our way into the Baltic Sea.

Our first stop was Gdansk, Poland. I remember this city as very bleak and gray. The people didn't smile. Blue jeans were a hot commodity and were sold on the "black market" for higher prices. We left Gdansk after one day. It was a place of turmoil and uprisings. The uprising occurred one week after we left Poland. Lech Walesa became a hero to the people when he co-founded the Solidarity Movement.[1] In 1983, he was given the Nobel Peace Prize, and in 1990, he became the president of Poland.[2] David and I left Poland with a desire to never return. But years later, I returned to Poland, and found a very different country. It was vibrant, and the people were very friendly and appeared to be quite happy.

We continued on to Russia, arriving in Leningrad, now known as St. Petersburg. When we disembarked from the ship we had to relinquish our passports to the authorities waiting at the end of the gangplank. We were then ushered to a security booth and were given special visas, which allowed us to enter the country. As we stood in front of the booth a gate closed shut on either side of us, trapping us in a small, tight area. It was rather frightening. After we passed through, we walked into the terminal. David watched as a returning citizen was being thoroughly searched. They took apart a TV that he had apparently brought home then tore apart his suitcase, strewing his clothes around before leaving him to put everything back together. It was very upsetting; this was not a pleasant introduction to Russia. Perhaps it is different today; I hope so. I have not returned to Russia since 1983.

A visit to the Hermitage was a must. The Hermitage is to Leningrad what the Louvre is to Paris. The colossal size of the Hermitage offered a phenomenal collection of great works of art. One of my favorites was the beautifully decorated Fabergé eggs.

In the evening, we went to the Palace of Culture and enjoyed a spectacular, energizing performance of a Russian dance troupe. I remember a comment that David made. "If I danced like that every day, I'd weigh only a hundred pounds." The dancers were so electrifying that one became exhausted watching them.

I recall an incident on the bus that was taking us to the performance. We had a young woman guide who involved us in a political conversation. Then, in a forceful tone, she stated, "Ve don't belief in God, ve belief in ourselves." Her statement sent shivers down my spine. I can almost hear her saying those words today.

Dance performance in Leningrad

Helsinki, Finland was our next port. We took a three-hour tour of the highlights of the city. We spent one day in Helsinki, and although it was quite interesting, it does not remain as memorable as some of the other ports of Scandinavia.

Stockholm, Sweden, was much more exciting and adventurous. I began to believe everyone in Sweden was blond. The Swedish people were delightful, warm and friendly, and the city was immaculate. We loved watching the little ones bathing naked in the square pool in the park. The children were beautiful.

Children bathing in the park on a hot summer day in Stockholm

Chess game in the park in Stockholm

The park seemed to be the place everyone congregated. Playing chess on a giant chessboard was a great pastime. One could spend an entire day dining, playing and relaxing in the park. David was an excellent chess player and stood watching them play. The young man who was playing observed David's interest in the game. He gestured to David to participate, but our group was leaving. David thanked him and suggested a move to the young man before departing. As we walked away, the young man shouted a hearty "thank you." Apparently, it was the right move.

We enjoyed wandering the streets, listening to the music of the street musicians, and watching the pomp and ceremony of the marching band.

The marching band in the park in Stockholm

We left Stockholm with a warm feeling and a desire to return someday.

Love this city . . . love this park. I'll be back.

On our way to Copenhagen we visited Odense, where Hans Christian Andersen was born in 1805. His former home is now a museum.

Upon entering the harbor in Copenhagen, one could not forget the charming fairy tales of Hans Christian Andersen. Sitting on a small clump of rocks, looking wistfully out to sea, is a beautiful statue of the "Little Mermaid," the tragic sea-girl who exchanged her voice for human legs, in order to gain the love of an earthly prince. When she was jilted, she threw herself into the sea and turned into foam. Because of my love of writing children's stories, the statue left a deep impression on me.

The Little Mermaid

When enjoying the benefits of a relaxing cruise, the only drawback is the lack of time to thoroughly visit each country. You get a taste of a country and are teased enough to draw you back for another land visit in the future, but cruising gives you the opportunity to visit places you may not necessarily plan to visit on a land trip. Again we had full days touring Copenhagen and travelling into the countryside, visiting its wondrous castles.

Egeskov was the highlight of all the castles. Having seen a number of castles in my lifetime, this one has always remained one of my favorites. The castle is still lived in-today, and the residents graciously allow tourism. It is one of Europe's best-preserved Renaissance water castles.

Egeskov Castle

Before returning to the ship, after an exciting, but long and tiring day, David and I stopped to rest at the Gefion Fountain on the harbor front. The fountain is the largest monument in Copenhagen, used as a wishing well. David and I threw our wishes into the tumbling water of the fountain, feeling so blessed for all the good fortune in our lives.

The last visit on our Baltic cruise brought us out into the North Atlantic Ocean to Oslo, Norway. I've always been an excellent sailor, but the North Atlantic did me in. While we were at sea the nausea was overwhelming until we reached port. There was a storm and the seas were extremely rough, more than usual. David was a captain of our own boats and was a true seafaring man. He weathered the storm quite well and tended to me through this difficult voyage.

Resting at the Gefion Fountain in Stockholm

Of all the sights that we enjoyed visiting on this fascinating cruise, the world famous Vigeland Sculpture Park remains the most outstanding. It is the largest sculpture park made by one single artist in the world.

This unique sculpture park is Gaston Vigeland's life work. There are 227 sculptures made of bronze, granite and wrought iron. His sculptures of people run the gamut from birth to youth to old age. I was deeply touched by Vigeland's sculptures, which evoked an emotional response to his stages of life. I can still visualize them today.

Entering Vigeland Park

Young Girls

Youth . . . young and strong

Young Couple—Courting

Aging

Old Age

The end of Vigeland Park

The Baltic Sea cruise is a must for anyone who loves cruising. Having enjoyed many Mediterranean trips, the Baltic, with its Scandinavian countries, was a very refreshing change.

1983, cruising the Baltic Sea on the *Vistafjord*

"The world is a book, and those who do not travel read only a page."
    —St. Augustine

TRAVEL: THE PASSION CONTINUES

TRAVELLING BECAME A GREAT adventure for David and me. We developed a curiosity and yearning to visit different cultures, different ways of life.

In 1988, we made a trip to Paris, Brussels, Bruges, Scotland, England and Wales.

Paris is an enchanting city, one that we loved exploring each time we visited. Both of us . . . born romantics . . . loved walking along the River Seine holding hands and exchanging kisses, lovers in our own romantic French movie.

The Louvre was always a treat, but the Musee d'Orsay was our favorite. We never tired of visiting this extraordinary museum.

The food, of course, was *magnifique*. We indulged our culinary passions more in Paris than in any other city we visited.

Leaving Paris, we flew to Brussels, a city we had never visited. Brussels is a "melting pot" with a unique character. Its culture is a cross between the Germanic in the North and the Romance in the South. We loved strolling along the beautiful squares and lunching outside, surrounded by deeply ornate buildings like the Grand Palace. The city has a renowned artist scene. The famous Belgian surrealist, René Magritte, studied in Brussels.

We took a delightful day trip to visit the city of Bruges, the capital and largest city of the province of West Flanders in the Flemish region of Belgium. Bruges reminded us of Amsterdam, as the city has many canals, and is often referred to as "The Venice of the North."[1]

A canal in Bruges

After leaving Belgium, we flew to London. David and I always loved London, and often took day trips into the countryside, enjoying the beautiful hills of the Cotswolds covered with golden-flowered buttercups. We had never explored the United Kingdom of Great Britain, and decided this was the perfect time to do it. We rented a car and drove north to Scotland through England's Lake District to begin our adventure. On the return trip we drove to Wales, and then took a train into London before departing for home.

Driving through the Lake District was a wondrous experience. It is a mountainous region in Northwest England, rife with streams, waterfalls and dales, and a popular vacation destination.

Leisurely driving for hours in this scenic wonderland was the perfect time to connect and reflect in conversation, discussing issues and anecdotes, which just brought us closer, and often made us laugh. I remember a conversation we had about our daughter, Tina, who we had been told, years before when she was a young teenager, was smoking pot. She had slept over a friend's house, and unbeknownst to us, her friend's mother had left for the weekend, leaving the girls home alone. The girl's mother returned home early and smelled the distinct aroma in her house. Furious, she sent Tina to walk home, and called us immediately. At the time, we were very disturbed and disciplined Tina. The day before we left on our trip, Tina, at the age of twenty-two and a "solid citizen," decided to tell us she had actually been smoking oregano at that time, and never felt a thing. Why she waited eight years to tell us, I'll never know. CHILDREN!!! David and I shared a good laugh.

Every marriage needs the opportunity to talk about issues in their lives in a peaceful environment, away from responsibilities, when one's heart, mind and soul are open to truly listening.

Our first stop, after arriving in the Lake District, was at the home of William Wordsworth, the nineteenth-century major Romantic English poet. Living in the Lake District, he was completely enraptured and inspired by the area, as was the artist Turner. Together with Samuel Taylor Coleridge, he helped launch the Romantic Age in English Literature.[2]

Wordsworth's first home was the *Dove Cottage* in Grasmere. He later moved to *Rydal Mount*, Ambleside.

Dove Cottage in Grasmere, home of William Wordsworth in the Lake District

Rydal Mount, Lake District, second home of William Wordsworth

Leaving the Lake District, we drove about another two hours before reaching Edinburgh, Scotland. After checking into the hotel, tired from the long drive, we decided to have dinner in the hotel dining room. We often enjoyed trying the local cuisine of a country whenever we travelled. Our waiter suggested we start with cock-a-leekie soup, followed by an appetizer of haggis. When we asked what haggis was, this is what we were told: sheep's stomach stuffed with minced offal (liver, heart and sometimes the lungs of an animal), oatmeal and suet.

My head said, "Yuck," but my mouth refrained from being insulting. I politely asked what other local specialties were offered. I stayed with the cock-a-leekie soup, which was quite good. David tried the haggis, but from the look on his face I was glad I didn't order it.

The following morning we awoke to a cool but sunny day. We were anxious to begin exploring Edinburgh, the capital of Scotland. There was so much to see in this beautiful city, and with only a few days to spend there, we decided to begin with Edinburgh Castle. The castle is the most famous of Scottish castles, and houses the Crown Jewels of Scotland, along with many historic relics. It also houses the National War Museum of Scotland.

Atop Edinburgh Castle

David at Edinburgh Castle in front of the dungeon

Watermill for torture

Edinburgh offered many excellent museums, which we thoroughly enjoyed, but of course, we set aside a few hours to shop on Princes Street in the New Town section of Edinburgh. The shops are on one side, and Edinburgh Castle rests across the street. David was always the shopper of the family; I couldn't keep up with him. Perhaps because he was in the garment manufacturing business, he always had his eyes open for the latest fashion. I was the guinea pig (excuse me . . . model) who had to try everything on.

Some of the famous residents of Edinburgh have included Charles Darwin; Sir Arthur Conan Doyle, who created *Sherlock Holmes*; J.K. Rowling, author of *Harry Potter*; Walter Scott, author of *Rob Roy* and *Ivanhoe*; and the notable Robert Louis Stevenson, creator of *Treasure Island* and the *Strange Case of Dr. Jekyll and Mr. Hyde.* Edinburgh has also been the home of Sean Connery, and is the hometown of former Prime Minister, Tony Blair.[3]

We left the mainland of Scotland and drove to meet the ferry, which took us to the Isle of Skye, the largest island in the Inner Hebrides of Scotland.[4] The ferry ride was invigorating in the cool crisp air.

We stayed in a charming bed and breakfast in the Sleat area of Skye. The beauty of Skye has been used as a location for a number of movies, including *Stardust*, with Robert De Niro. Jethro Tull owned an estate on Skye and wrote songs about the Isle.[5]

We enjoyed a delightful day on the water with a small group of people. We left the dock at Elgol and proceeded to Loch Coruisk in the Cuillin Hills. We encountered a large colony of seals, and later sighted a few sharks, but no whales, and loved watching the dolphins that enjoyed swimming alongside the boats. It reminded us of the years we lived in Florida when we sailed our boat down the Intracoastal Waterway. We loved watching the dolphins swimming alongside us, leaping and frolicking.

After our boat trip in the late afternoon, we drove to a fudge and chocolate company in Dunvegan, which offered samples of the many varieties of fudge and chocolate it produced. After the tenth tasting, I was so satiated, I skipped dinner and opted for a cup of tea.

We left Skye the following day, returning to the mainland aboard the ferry, and proceeded on our return journey through northern England, crossing the Scotland/England border. We soon came upon Hadrian's Wall, one of the most important monuments built by the Romans in Britain. We walked along the wall a great distance.

Continuing on our journey, we found an old castle that was open for guest accommodations. Since we had a long journey ahead of us, we decided to stay overnight. I felt like a princess back in the 1500s.

The drive to reach Wales was again a joy, stopping in quaint towns along the way. We arrived in Wales in the evening, and had to stop at a hotel to ask directions, as the signs were very difficult to read. It was a bit nerve-wracking, as there were few lights along the way. We finally arrived at our destination, a lovely thatched roof inn.

The following day we went into the town of Llangollen. It had turned raw and cold. Before leaving the town to head back to the inn, I peered into a shop window. The window had a collection of the cutest pencils I had ever seen. They were designed to look like people.

We returned to the inn, cold and hungry. The innkeeper placed us in front of the fireplace with blankets over our knees, and brought us dinner on tray tables so we could enjoy the warmth of the fire. I was so inspired by those adorable pencils that I sat in front of the fireplace and wrote one of my favorite stories about little pencil people.

We left the car in Wales, after another day of touring, and headed back to London on the train. Two more days in London ended this unforgettable voyage. Again, we enjoyed the many cultures . . . different, and yet in many ways similar to our own. The world is not always as foreign as we assume, once we allow ourselves to understand other societies.

IN 1989, THE LAST YEAR of the decade, we decided to travel to Hawaii, instead of going abroad. It was a great decision, as the beauty of the Islands of Hawaii offer so much to enjoy. We chose to visit the Big Island of Hawaii and Maui.

On the Big Island we took a helicopter ride, which took us over most of the island. The pilot flew us over an inactive volcano thousands of years old, and then proceeded to fly us over a live volcano. I sat next to the pilot on this scary adventure. When we reached the live volcano he dipped the nose of the craft, perhaps a hundred feet above the boiling cauldron, and hovered over it for a few minutes. It was an amazing sight. We could actually feel the heat.

Live Volcano

He then flew us over a town that had been completely covered by the lava from a major eruption.

A town completely covered by lava. The only remaining sign of existence was the STOP sign with the street signs above it.

We continued flying over the island to enjoy more of the sites and the beauty. Then the pilot turned toward the ocean and we saw more of the volcanic activity.

Lava flowing into the ocean from a live volcano

It was a thrilling experience, but I was delighted to return to the safety of solid ground.

A safe return

We left the island of Hawaii, after a wonderful few days, and went to Kapalua Bay on Maui, another beautiful island.

Outside our room was an inviting lagoon. Although I am no longer an avid swimmer, the lagoon, with its warm water, beckoned me. It was like floating in a warm bathtub. This was the most romantic place on the trip. We sat on the beach in front of our suite in the early evening, watching the sunset and drinking champagne.

We loved our trip and hoped to return to the islands someday.

Once you have travelled, the voyage never ends, but is played out over and over again in the quietest chambers. The mind can never break off from the dream.
—Pat Conroy

THE ERA OF THE 1990s remains etched in my memory. Birth, death, tragedy, joy... it was rife with all the conditions of life.

In June, 1991, our second grandchild, Josh, was born; four days later, our third grandchild, Alex, arrived... two precious little boys. In December, 1993, Josh's brother, Brad, was born. We were now blessed with four grandchildren.

Life is a balancing act. I sometimes visualize the masks of comedy and tragedy, which have their origin in Greek Theater. The masks have endured for centuries, reflecting the twin themes of joy and despair of the human condition.

In January, 1994, my father died. We were in the midst of building our dream house. The following year, in April, 1995, while preparing to move into the new house, my husband, David, broke his neck. In December, 1996, my mother passed away.

Fortunately, in the last few years of the 90s, life normalized; we were able to pursue our love of travelling again.

From 1990 to 2000, our travels took us to many countries. I will share the highlights of our adventures of the early 90s, as my voyages could fill their own book.

I do not wish my life to appear as a travelogue. I have been a globetrotter, a sightseer, a voyager, an explorer and a roamer but I am a journeyer. Life is a journey, an adventure. I have been living the adventure from the day I was born, and I will continue to do so till life ceases.

HIGHLIGHTS OF THE EARLY 1990s

IN MAY, 1990, WE EMBARKED on an adventurous driving trip throughout France. We began in Paris, and drove to Rouen, the Cathedral City of France, for a day visit, then continued on to Giverny, the home of the artist, Monet. The gardens were outstanding.

There were so many species of flowers, but the lovely water lilies floating in the pond were reminiscent of his famous paintings.

The Gardens at Giverny

After leaving Giverny, we drove north to Honfleur on the Normandy Coast. We arrived at the renowned Ferme St. Simeon, a gracious manor house, in time for dinner. We remained for two relaxing days, and then continued following the coast of Normandy, stopping in Deauville for a few hours.

The Manor House at Ferme St. Simeon in Honfleur

Our next accommodation, the Chateau D'Audrieu, was an imposing, five-star estate with lovely, majestic gardens.

Chateau D'Audrieu

Gardens of Chateau D'Audrieu

Arronmanches and Utah Beach, the Great War memorials, were in close proximity. The story of the Allied landing of the D-Day invasion of Normandy, in June 1944, was shown on film in the museum. David and I were very young when WWII was over, and compared with seeing documentaries depicting the war, being at the actual site of the invasion and visiting the graves of our fallen young men profoundly affected us. I remember being in camp the summer of 1944, when celebrations broke out throughout the area, commemorating the end of the war. Did I realize the extent and significance of what was happening? As a child I believe I was influenced by the effect it had on my parents. I doubt I understood the full meaning of it all.

On a more upbeat note, we travelled to the HIGHLIGHT of the trip, Mont St Michel, on the Normandy Coast. The rocky island of Mont St Michel was once a Benedictine Abbey. We lodged at Mère Poulard, an old hotel in the middle of the town. Getting onto Mont St Michel was quite tricky, as it could only be reached by a narrow causeway from the mainland. The high tide came in late afternoon, and if you didn't reach Mont St Michel before the tide swept over the road and created an island, separating it from the mainland, you did not reach Mont St Michel. The tide rushed in so swiftly that if you were on the road, the car would be swept away. We also heard many stories of pedestrians carried away in the tide.

Mont St Michel

The hotel, Mère Poulard, had a charming restaurant with a famous kitchen, open to the public on the main street. The attraction was the chef beating the dough in a copper bowl like the rhythm on a drum. My husband, David, was so fascinated that he asked if he could beat the dough. The chef taught him, and suddenly there was a crowd watching this American beat the dough to a rhythmic cadence. We got to enjoy the omelette David had prepared.

The kitchen of Mère Poulard

We left Mont St Michel (during low tide!) and continued driving south along the Brittany Coast, stopping in St. Malo for lunch. We finally arrived at Les Sorinières, staying at the beautiful Abbaye de Villineuve, a thirteenth-century abbey.

From Les Sorinières, we then drove to Nieuil and stayed at the Chateau-Hôtel de Nieuil, an old castle turned into a hotel in 1937. Originally, it was a hunting lodge of King Francis I.

Our trip ended abruptly, after arriving at Relais Margeaux. There was an emergency phone message from my brother at home, which required our immediate return to the States. My mother had been hospitalized with congestive heart failure. We left the following morning at six a.m. from a small country airport. Driving the coastline of France was magnificent and adventurous. It was a glorious trip, and fortunately the situation at home, which was life-threatening at the time, turned out well.

JULY, 1990—WE JOINED MY COUSINS on a cruise aboard the *Dawn Princess* to Alaska, sailing from Vancouver through the inside passage and arriving the following day in Ketchikan, the "Salmon Capital of the World."

We visited ports, including Juneau and Skagway, and travelled to many of the important cities of Alaska.

The <u>HIGHLIGHT</u> of the trip was flying over the glaciers and landing at Taku Glacier Lodge, for the best salmon bake we had ever had. I still enjoy the recipe today.

The trip over the glacier was very unsettling, as the weather had turned bad. We flew in a five passenger plane with a *real* "bush pilot," who assured us we would arrive safely after dropping possibly a hundred feet over a glacier. It was worth it! But, we should never have taken off in that weather. My cousin became hysterical and kept repeating, "We're going to die." When we finally arrived, she was taken to the lodge to rest, as she was too upset to eat.

While having lunch, we saw a bear resting on the barbecue grill where the salmon was cooked. He was enjoying the leftover scraps that dropped onto the coals, placing his paw down through the grill to reach every last morsel. I ran outside, standing less than fifteen feet away, and took this picture.

The bear enjoying a freebie lunch

In Anchorage, we boarded the Midnight Sun Express to Denali National Park, viewing some of Alaska's most spectacular scenery and the great wildlife preserve. We ventured to take a rafting trip through the rapids, and saw the aeries (nests) of the bald eagles. We also were able to view Mt. McKinley within a few miles, the tallest mountain in the United States.

Our trip was enjoyable and informative, but a trip to Alaska is a one-time visit.

IN MAY, 1992, WE TRAVELLED to Spain with our dear friends, Joe and Joan. Joe, born in Nicaragua, was fluent in Spanish, and with David's fluency in Spanish, we travelled well.

We arrived in Madrid to beautiful weather, and enjoyed the sites of the city within a few days. The Spanish paella was excellent, better than at our local restaurant at home.

Continuing on to Cordoba, we visited the Cathedral of Cordoba, where Pablo de Céspedes' famous painting *Last Supper* hangs.

Standing below *Last Supper*

The next city on our travels, Granada, was the <u>HIGHLIGHT</u> of the trip through Spain.

We stayed at the Parador de Granada San Francisco; the hotel is a fifteenth-century convent and part of the Palace of Alhambra.

The Alhambra of Granada rises upon the hill of La Sabica and dominates the entire city. I remember looking across to the other side from my room. There were caves tucked into the rocky hills, and people were living in the caves. A tour guide mentioned that at times throughout the years, lepers had inhabited the caves.

The Alhambra was one of the most beautiful places we had ever visited. Below are photographs displaying the beauty of this place.

The beautiful scenes of the Alhambra

Seville was the next stop on our journey. It was alive with excitement of the Expo'92, a world expo represented by over a hundred countries. The theme of the expo was "The Age of Discovery."

Expo'92 in Seville

I recall a very funny incident one evening when David and Joe waited on line for the bus to return us to the hotel from the Expo. Joan and I sat resting on a stone wall. Behind David were two older women standing on line. Joe told David to say something to them in Spanish. Although David was quite fluent in the language, he didn't understand Joe's suggested comment. Assuming it was okay, David repeated the comment to the women. The two women began to blush and started giggling. David asked Joe what he had just repeated. The answer had a very sexual content, which does not bear repeating. David wanted to *kill* Joe. When the two of them got together they were like children, always laughing and joking with each other. David composed himself, after turning red, and apologized to the women.

We continued travelling through the south of Spain after leaving our friends, and crossed the border of Spain into Portugal. We drove to the Algarve and arrived at our hotel, the Boa Vista in Albufeira. I remember the magnificent view of the sea from our room. David was a Pisces, and loved anything on the water. There was something about the sea that turned David into a "Don Juan." How lucky could I get?

After a few restful days, we continued driving north through Portugal. We reached Lisbon, the capital and largest city in Portugal, set on seven hills. We spent a few days wandering the city, enjoying the museums, and dining at the charming cafes, and restaurants. We left Portugal, heading home, with a warm feeling for the entire Iberian Peninsula.

In October, 2011, I returned to Spain with my son, Cliff, and daughter-in-law, Nancy, after nineteen years. I had many stories to share with them.

LONDON WAS ALWAYS our favorite "stopping off" city when returning to the States, after visiting countries in Europe; it was the shortest distance home.

In 1993, we decided to fly to London for a short visit to enjoy the theater, shopping and just roaming around the city we loved. After a few days, David announced he had a surprise for me. The surprise was a trip to Portofino; we had never been there, but it was on our list of places we wanted to visit.

Portofino became the _HIGHLIGHT_ of our short visit. This beautiful, half moon-shaped, seaside village is on the Italian Riviera. Pastel houses line the entrance to the harbor. We stayed at the Hotel Splendido, which sits high above the village overlooking the sea. Portofino is truly a paradise; it's reported to be one of the loveliest Mediterranean seaports. I would not tire of visiting this exquisite village again.

The entrance to the harbor of Portofino

The beautiful Hotel Splendido

Our "short visit" turned into a memorable experience. *Thank you David.*

Twenty years from now you will be more disappointed by the things you didn't do than by the ones you did do. So throw off the bowlines, sail away from the safe harbor, catch the trade wind in your sails. Explore. Dream. Discover.

—H. Jackson Brown, Jr., *P.S. I Love You (Brown attributed the quote to his mother)*

HIGHLIGHT OF 1996

WOULD MY LIFE WITH DAVID ever be the same? Six months, from April, 1995 to October, David remained home, struggling each day to become the strong, vibrant man he was before the horrific accident that broke his neck. He finally returned to work a few days a week that October. Early in January of 1996, he came home after work one day and announced, "I'm retiring. Life is too short and I've been given another chance."

In May, 1996, after a three year hiatus, including a year of David's recuperation from a broken neck, we were anxious to spread our wings. David was back! We flew to Paris, one of our most romantic cities, and stayed for two days at a charming hotel, Relais Christine, on the Left Bank. We visited our favorite sites and dined at restaurants we had never been to before. *I wonder if Paris has a bad restaurant?* On the third day, we began our adventurous driving trip through France.

We drove out of Paris en route to Fère-en-Tardenois, west of Reims which is about an hour's drive from Paris, and arrived at our destination, the Chateau de Fère, a storybook chateau with the ruins of a fourteenth-century castle on the grounds.

Ruins of a fourteenth-century castle at Chateau de Fère

In the early afternoon, we set out to visit the Moet-Chandon winery and caves in Epernay. We were champagne lovers and were fascinated by the interesting facts we learned about the process of making champagne and what makes certain grapes excellent for champagne—chalk in the earth.

Before saying goodbye to the beautiful chateau, we enjoyed an excellent Sunday brunch. Everywhere we travelled in France, the food was a joy to the palate.

Sunday brunch at Chateau de Fère

The weather, since we arrived in France, had been very unpredictable: one day sunshine, one day rain. We awoke to a sunny day when we left Chateau de Fère and headed for Esclimont, stopping at Vaux-le-Viscomte, a marvelous chateau with a great history. La Fontaine, the famous children's author of fables, had lived there. This was of great interest to me, as I loved writing children's stories with a moral. I sometimes imagined myself as Aesop in a former life. Many of my stories seemed to emerge as fables.

Wax figures of the fables of La Fontaine at Vaux-le-Viscomte

We visited the Chateau de Fontainebleau for the second time, then went into the village of Fontainebleau and stopped at the local bakery for a luscious pastry with bottled water for our lunch, and then continued driving to Esclimont. Probably, most people never get to visit the village; it's a charming place.

Awesome is definitely a good description of Chateau Esclimont. Built in 1543, the castle is surrounded by ponds inhabited by swans and lovely gardens. The grounds were so magnificent; they induced us to take a long walk the following day in the refreshing morning air. David reminded me of the beauty of our home in Connecticut. Our house was our "castle," with magnificent gardens, and we even had a pair of swans that visited us in the morning on our lake. Swans mate forever. How lucky we were!

Chateau Esclimont

After a most relaxing visit at this exquisite chateau, we left Esclimont, heading towards Chartres and Chambord. I kept watching David for signs of exhaustion; I didn't want to tire him. But, he had more energy than I did. He came alive again, enjoying every moment, every day.

We continued our trip, crossing the Loire River into the Loire Valley, the breathtaking countryside and valley of the Royal Chateaux.

I was taken aback by the enormous size of Chambord, which loomed ahead of us. Chambord was the majestic 440-room hunting haunt of Francois I. This trip was turning into a "castle tour," but we loved it. Travelling again with my handsome "Romeo" was a gift.

David in front of Chambord

Continuing our incredible journey, we arrived in Onzain before 7:00 p.m., at Domain des Hautes de Loire. The weather warmed up again, close to the eighties, after being quite cool; it was a beautiful evening. Our *superior* room had a problem, so we were moved to a deluxe suite with a terrace and a HUGE bathroom. *Magnifique!* Our son, Todd, and our daughter-in-law, Diane, had stayed here and recommended it to us. They were right on!

The following morning was an amazing experience visiting many of the chateaus of the Loire. The Loire is truly the land of kings, queens and castles. We weren't able to visit all of them; the temperature reached ninety-eight degrees at one point. Tomorrow, we decided, we would visit some we had missed before heading for Vezelay. I have seen many chateaus and castles in my travels, but I believe France surpasses every country in the amount and magnificence of these structures.

On to Villandry. We visited only the spectacular gardens. I had never seen any comparable in all of Europe. They were designed for different areas of use: a kitchen garden of vegetables and herbs, a medicinal garden, a flowers and shrub garden, et al. The ornamental gardens were given different names: "The tragedy of Love;" "The fickleness of Love;" "The tenderness of Love;" "The folly of Love." What could they possibly grow to enhance the quality of *Love*? Leave it to the French to grow a garden with the intent of promoting LOVE. God bless them!

The gardens of Villandry

Next, we visited Chinon, the ruins of the castle where Joan of Arc visited the Dauphin before he became king, to beg him to allow her to lead an army to rid France of the Britons.

We decided to head back to Onzain, as it was almost 6:00 p.m. and very hot.

Tomorrow was another day! Wine and dinner on the terrace brought the end to a beautiful day. But the final end of the evening was influenced by the ornamental gardens of *Love* in Villandry.

We left early the following morning on our way to Vezelay. It was

The floating chateau of Chenonceau

overcast with a drop in the temperature of about twenty-five degrees. We stopped to visit Chenonceau, which spans the River Cher, resting on a group of arches with the river flowing beneath it.

The town of Vezelay, in Burgundy, startles one at the approach. It rises out of the earth, high on a hill and majestic in the early evening light. In all of France there is possibly no village of its tiny size with a past like Vezelay. It has a remarkable religious history dating back to the eighth century.

Just outside Vezelay is the world-famous L'Esperance, Marc Meneau's restaurant. Across from his renowned restaurant, we were accommodated in a lovely room at his Pré des Marguerites.

If I had to choose a highlight of a dinner I have had in all my travels, it would be the following: an aperitif (champagne) before the main meal, a vegetable tart—a high, thin crater of a tart filled with fresh vegetables served for two *enormous* people, and roasted turbot—a fish (whole), about four pounds, that had to be eaten in two separate servings. The dinner was indescribable. It was a gastronomist's orgy. I had never eaten that much food in one sitting in my life.

David asked Marc Meneau to join us after dinner. What a delightful man! David was interested in the possibility of importing Marc Meneau's wine. We spoke for about an hour, but the complications of importing the wine deterred David from pursuing it.

We left Vezeley after a lovely breakfast in L'Esperance and headed for Gilly. The weather was cool and cloudy, which made it an easy driving day of about two and a half hours.

We arrived at Chateau Gilly late afternoon. An enormous, ancient, limestone castle greeted us; it had been a monastery. It was quite simple but elegant.

On Saturday afternoon we went into the lovely town of Beaune; the shopkeepers were friendly and very helpful. I bought David a beautiful summer robe and a magnifying mirror for my dressing table in a charming bath shop. We visited an excellent wine store and brought back some of our favorite wines, in demi-bottles, to our room. We didn't make it to dinner that evening and had dinner sent to our room . . . in bed.

Sunday morning was rainy, about sixty degrees; we decided to have breakfast in the room. On our way back to Beaune to visit the famous Hotel-Dieu, an historic hospital built in 1443, the rain stopped. The Hospices de Beaune, as it was known, was a hospice for the poor, perfectly preserved. Countless sick were taken in and cared for by the nuns. The design was magnificent, with multicolored tiled roofs. The interior was beautiful, with separate enclosed beds similar to a large sleeping compartment on a train, draped in red velvet. David discovered the wine that the nuns produced each year and fell in love with it, but couldn't purchase it at the time.

Leaving Beaune the following morning, we continued south, lunching at a local restaurant in Cluny. We continued driving, reaching Perouges mid-afternoon. The hotel was situated inside the walled city of Perouges in a small square. The city dated back to the thirteenth century. And all the edifices looked it! The streets were heavily cobblestoned. For many years, when we came to France, we headed for Paris and its environs. Our trip on the coastline of this incredible country, and now travelling through the interior, was an exciting adventure. The flavor of the country really came through. The people, the customs and the atmosphere were very different from the big cities. It almost felt as if we were in a different country.

Our room had charming, old, double canopy beds with a huge limestone fireplace, but no TV and no air-conditioning. It was so quiet one could hear a pin drop. Perouges was a perfect example of a city from the middle ages. Because of our reservation at the hotel, we were entitled to drive into the walled city. Dining in the restaurant felt as if we were dining in the fifteenth century; the waitresses wore lace caps and lace ruffled, crisp white aprons but the food was definitely twentieth-century. We were told that President Clinton and his wife were due to arrive that week.

After an overnight stay, we had breakfast in the square before we left Perouges and continued driving into the heart of Provence.

Breakfast in Perouges

Driving through the French Alps, the weather was gray with a mist hiding much of the great heights. The sun began to play peek-a-boo before we entered the town of Serres in the Hautes-Alpes. We stopped for lunch at the small Hotel Fifi Moulin. Finally, the sun stopped playing games and the temperature began rising into the seventies. Time seemed to disappear, so we proceeded through Nyons onto Vaison-la-Romaine.

Stopping in Vaison-la-Romaine was quite interesting; the town held many ancient ruins. We wanted to spend more time in this picturesque, charming town, but heat prodded us onward; the trip proved exhausting, driving on narrow, winding mountain roads. We finally arrived in Nimes early evening; the trip was close to nine hours.

We checked into the hotel, but were very unhappy with the hotel and the accommodations. David called our New York agent to see what he could do. We lucked out! Our agent was able to get us into the Jules Cesar in Arles—originally our first choice hotel, but it had been booked. We quickly left Nimes heading for Arles, arriving around 9:00 p.m. We went straight to dinner, a six course gastronomic delight, and then to bed.

The room was a welcome site after Nimes; the Jules Cesar is a five-star hotel in Arles—a wonderful small city.

After breakfast on the patio, we wandered though town and found a children's store, and couldn't resist *dropping a bundle* for the grandchildren.

Dinner that evening was very special. David found the wine he had loved when we were in Beaune. Once a year, the nuns auctioned their wine internationally. A very small amount is made and it is very difficult to get, as we were told the Japanese buy up most of it each year. David ordered a demi-bottle of 1973 Hospice de Beaune for himself. I wasn't interested. "May I take a sip?" I asked. Then I drank half the glass as it was soooo good.

"HONEY!!" he cried. "All you wanted was a sip." Then he quickly ordered a second bottle. *It was incredible!*

We ventured out of Arles the following day, visiting Les Beaux, a village high on a rock spur half mile long, built in medieval times. We lunched in a small outdoor cafe, and strolled through the ancient village. The temperature soared towards ninety degrees, so we headed back to Arles for a dip in the

swimming pool.

We left Arles the next day, on our way to Èze, and stopped in Aix-en Provence, another ancient city. Aix is the heart of Provence, and a charming walking city.

The beautiful tree-lined main street of Aix-en-Provence

It was nearing lunchtime, and I had brought with me an article from *Traveler Magazine* about a great restaurant in Aix-en Provence. We found the restaurant on the main street and decided we would dine there. We entered and were offered a seat on the main floor. We asked for the manager, as that was not the room in the photograph in the magazine. The owner greeted us with a warm welcome, and explained that the room was closed during the day. I showed him the article from the magazine and explained we were looking forward to dining in the magnificent room while we were in Aix. He was so delighted, that he opened the room for us, sent us complimentary drinks, and we had a lovely lunch in our own private dining room.

Dining in Aix-en Provence (Our own private dining room)

On our way to Èze, formerly a medieval town, the temperature became very hot. Down along the Côte D'Azur (French Riviera) the Mediterranean lolled beneath the majestic mountains that rose along the coast and swept down to the sea. Only one road led to the small village of Èze, as we travelled the middle road of the Grand Corniche. From the main road the car climbed the mountain into the ancient village at its bottom. We then walked the stone streets to our hotel, the Chateau Eza, high above us on the edge of the cliffs. The luggage was pushed up on carts all the way to the top. *Poor porter!*

The Swedish Royal Family was the original owner of the hotel. There were only ten rooms, and each room was decorated differently. Our room (the Chambre De Jardin or the garden room) was exquisite, with a wrought iron canopy bed with silk flowers running up the poles of the bed and across the canopy. I felt like I was sleeping in a garden or a brothel. The room was a honeymooner's dream. *Vive le plaisir.*

A small terrace with a table and chairs opened out from the bedroom. Dinner was on the terrace below our bedroom with the same breathtaking view.

Breakfast on the terrace the following morning was . . . indescribable. I had never viewed the Mediterranean from that height. The coastline was so picturesque, the view recalled scenes from the movies. The chateau clings to the side of the ancient rock walls of Èze, more than 1,300 feet above the Mediterranean.

We walked down from the hotel that morning . . . *easy.* Walking back up . . . WHEW!

View from our terrace at Chateau Eza

Another hot day and it was goodbye France, hello Italy. We're off to Portofino on the autoroute, high above the coast, through the mountains and tunnels, which cut into the seacoast mountains almost all the way.

We were thrilled to revisit Portofino, after being there in 1993. We had pledged to return. And we did. We returned to London for our trip home, after a few days of enjoying Portofino. In London, the following day, we walked to the Speaker's Corner in Hyde Park and listened to the rhetoric being espoused by some of the world's "madmen." It was time to go home.

I struggled to choose the highlight of this incredible journey, and I realized the _HIGHLIGHT_ of this trip and of 1996 was David. I had my husband back . . . strong, whole and well again. There was no better highlight than that.

Like all great travelers, I have seen more than I remember, and remember more than I have seen.
    —Benjamin Disraeli

In June of 1997, the daughter of our dear friends, Joe and Joan, was married on the lawn of their Fort Lee, New Jersey home on the Hudson River, overlooking New York City. The groom, whom the bride had met in New York, was from Rome.

The reception was tented on the lawn; it was the most festive wedding I had ever attended. Family and friends from Italy were exuberant; the Italians are so full of life. The parents of the groom were making another wedding reception, two weeks later, at their country house in Lake Bracciano, an hour outside of Rome. We decided to combine this beautiful occasion with an exciting adventure exploring Italy.

EXPLORING ITALY

DAVID AND I LEFT NEW YORK for Italy, which proved to be a thoroughly enjoyable and memorable trip. We had enjoyed roaming through France, and this gave us the opportunity to amble our way through Italy.

We arrived in Milan, and after renting a car at the airport, we were on our way to Sirmione, a beautiful, tropical peninsula jutting into Lake Garda. We reached Sirmione, a walled city, around noon and received permission from the local police to drive through. Because we were booked at the Hotel Villa Cortine Palace, we were permitted to drive the car through this old, narrow city with a castle in the center of town. It was difficult to drive through the narrow streets; we had to maneuver the car between the pedestrians.

Once we were outside the main business district, we proceeded on till we reached the high gates of Villa Cortine, a magnificent villa built in the early 1900s. The long winding drive up to the hotel was through the villa's palatial park.

After checking into our room, we headed to their beach for a dip in the water and a barbecue buffet lunch. It was hot! After lunch we returned to the room for a siesta till 7:00 p.m.; we were exhausted. We dined outside on our terrace overlooking the lake. The weather had cooled a little in the early evening. We listened to the music of Andrea Bocelli. I believe his album *Romanza* was playing. *Romanza* was definitely on our "menu" that evening.

The following morning we repeated our pleasurable dining experience and had breakfast on the terrace, enjoying the view of the lake.

We remained for only one night at this lovely villa, and then left for Montecatini, with an interesting stop in the city of Verona, a city with great history. Verona was the home of Romeo and Juliet. We visited the famous balcony belonging to the Capulet family, and then strolled through the city with its charming shops and outdoor cafes.

Juliet's balcony

We arrived in Montecatini Terme, a jewel set in the hills of Tuscany, at about 5:00 p.m. Our hotel, the Grand Hotel e la Pace, was set in a park, and inhabited an entire city block. Our corner room faced the mountains with the old village atop the rear hills. We took a stroll through this elegant small city, and then returned for a drink at the bar before dinner. We dined at a local restaurant, and I found my favorite fish again: St. Peter's fish, the one I had enjoyed in Israel.

The following morning we awoke to another beautiful day. After breakfast we headed for Collodi to visit the Pinocchio Park. Carlo Lorenzi, the author of *Pinocchio*, adopted the name Carlo Collodi, after the village where his mother was born. It was a delightful experience seeing many of the fabulous bronze and steel sculptures of the characters from *Pinocchio*, and a live puppet show for the children. David commented that our grandchildren would have loved the park; it was a child's paradise. I believe we all remain children at heart. He also let me know he was keeping an eye on my nose. If it grew longer he would know what was behind it. David was a great tease . . . but I loved it!

The steel sculpture of the whale from Pinocchio

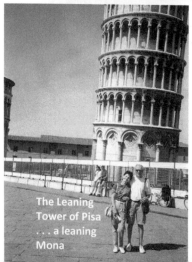

The Leaning Tower of Pisa . . . a leaning Mona

We travelled on to Pisa, to visit the famous leaning tower. Every year since 1178 A.D., only five years after the tower was built, it has continued to lean one to two millimeters a year. It had recently been shored up with concrete blocks to counterbalance the leaning.

We then drove to the seashore of Viareggio, savoring an invigorating breath of sea air from the Gulf of Genoa. We walked along the beach for a respite from the continuous driving, and then headed back to Montecatini.

After dinner, we took a leisurely walk through the busy streets; it was a balmy night and everyone strolls late evening, including *bambinos* in their carriages.

In the morning, we left for Siena, with a stop for lunch in San Gimignano, a charming hilltop city, famed for its towers. The restaurant is on top of a tower overlooking the city and the Tuscan hills, draped in olive groves and vineyards. What a glorious sight!

On our way to Siena on the Autostrada, we missed our exit and had to take the next exit, winding our way back through the maze of this small city of almost sixty thousand people. On the outskirts of the city, our hotel sat perched on a hilltop overlooking the city, in a park-like setting.

We taxied into town for dinner at a local restaurant, Da Papei. They had excellent Tuscan food, right off the Piazza del Campo, where the famous Palio is held twice a year. (Palio is the horse race run around the huge, fan-shaped piazza.)

The Piazza del Campo, where the Palio is held

The Palio involves ten horses and riders, riding barebacked and dressed in the color representing their *Contrade,* or city ward.

Dinner that evening was most enjoyable, as we dined outside and met a young couple from Tempe, Arizona, and spent the evening chatting till about 11:00 p.m. They were on their honeymoon and were so delighted to talk to an older couple who had been married for "so long." They wanted to know our *secret*. I let David answer that one.

The next day was spent shopping in Siena, searching for gifts for the children and getting the feel of this very old city dating back to the 1200s.

The following day was Sunday, Father's Day. We awoke early, had breakfast, and started our tip to Orvieto, arriving early afternoon. Our hotel in Orvieto was an ancient monastery, originally begun in the eighth century. The monastery was on a hill, high on volcanic rock, facing the walled city of Orvieto across the valley, a ten-minute car ride.

After lunch, we were a little travel-weary, so we opted to relax around the pool on a very hot afternoon, planning to visit the city later in the day. Retuning to the room around 3:00 p.m., to call the children, we fell asleep, and awoke in time for dinner. Sorry kids. No phone call.

After a great night's sleep, a light breakfast and a delightful chat with a couple from Melbourne, Australia—they had been married longer than us— we were on our way to Positano.

Early afternoon, we arrived in Positano, a cliffside resort nestled into the rock at the edge of the Gulf of Salerno. The ride to our hotel, San Pietro, was a winding road cut into the cliffs, high above Positano. The entrance, when one arrives, is nothing more than a few small structures. The porter took our bags down some stone steps to an elevator. Then, *voila,* the San Pietro, an exquisite gem overlooking the sea, appeared. There were gardens everywhere—glass enclosed rooms—a paradise. Our room was on a landing all by itself, with a terrace overlooking the water. We lunched on a semi-outdoor terrace enjoying pasta and swordfish. The hotel is an architectural wonder, cleverly tucked into the cliffs in a series of nearly a dozen ledges, each one-room width, so that every room is perfectly private, with its own balcony and magnificent view.

A room in San Pietro overlooking the view

One of the lovely terraces

The multi ledges of the Hotel San Pietro

After taking a tour of this breathtaking hotel, we decided to go into Positano and have dinner at the Hotel Palazzo Murat, a restaurant suggested by the maître d' at our hotel. It was an excellent choice. Walking through Positano in the early evening, we worked our way down to the beach, where the television crew was filming a contest of the top models of the world. Everything in Positano was quite steep—either up or down, including my husband's eyes, while he was enjoying the sight of those gorgeous models.

The next day, Tuesday, June 17th . . . MY BIRTHDAY! It was another glorious day. We opted for breakfast on our terrace then went down to the terraced beach for some R&R.

Later that day, we returned to Positano for lunch overlooking the beach, where we continued to watch the filming of the models, which had been going on for days. After lunch, David suggested we go down to the beach. I said, "NO, let's go shopping." I was not going to let him ogle those beauties again.

My birthday dinner that night was marvelous . . . the best chateaubriand I ever had. Next to our table, I recognized a well-known actor from a long-running TV show, enjoying dinner with his wife. Then I also realized their room was next to ours, as I heard them chatting on their terrace when I was sitting on ours. Two summers ago in Manhattan, I was dining with a friend at an outdoor restaurant. I recognized the same actor sitting next to my table. I politely asked him if he remembered being in Positano in 1997. He was so delighted that I brought up the subject; we spoke for a while, recalling that beautiful memory. When he got up to leave, he came to my table, asked me to rise, and gave me a big hug and said, "Till we meet again."

A view of Positano from San Pietro

On Wednesday, we took the boat out of Positano to Capri, our second visit to this enchanting place. It was a very enjoyable day visiting Capri again. Memories of our first trip to Capri came flooding back. I was still wearing the ring that David had bought me at La Perla. We took the funicular up to the village of Capri, stopping at some of the shops we had liked previously. We taxied to a restaurant for lunch in Anacapri, a small village above Capri, on the other side of the island, and then dropped down to the restaurant just above the Blue Grotto. Quite a trip! We retuned to Positano on a jet boat in record time.

We discovered a delicious, refreshing drink called "limoncello," a lemon alcoholic drink that we developed a taste for. It's kept in the freezer, like vodka. *Molto benne!*

Our last night at San Pietro, we dined on the terrace of the hotel dining room. We met an adorable young couple from Manhattan on their honeymoon. What was it about honeymooners that were drawn to us? Did we look or act like honeymooners, or did we appear to be a romantic older couple, which appealed to the senses of these young people? The atmosphere was so conducive for casual conversation, as there were so many Americans there and everyone was very friendly.

Positano and the Hotel San Pietro was the <u>*HIGHLIGHT*</u> of this marvelous trip. If I were ever given the choice to return to one place in the world, it would be here.

The next morning, we began our trip to Fiuggi on our way back to Rome, stopping in Pompeii. What an experience! Pompeii was the largest Roman ruins of a city I had ever seen, founded in 8 B.C.E.; it was buried in 79 C.E. by the eruption of Mt. Vesuvius. We spent close to three hours there and lunched in a restaurant in the middle of the vast ruins. It was brutally hot!

We continued driving, arriving in Fiuggi for an overnight stay before starting out for Rome in the morning, stopping at the airport to drop off the car. Our hotel in Rome had a car pick us up at the airport and we got to our hotel before noon. We decided to visit with our friends, Joe and Joan, since they had arrived earlier from the States. Leaving the hotel that evening, David had stepped outside to get a taxi; I followed shortly after. As I walked through the lobby, I saw a tall, handsome man walking towards me. I suddenly realized it was Andrea Bocelli. I was paralyzed. I stood there staring at him, aware he could not see me, as he passed very close to me.

Pompeii

When I reached David outside the hotel, I could barely speak. Relating to David who I had just seen, he was very disappointed that he had missed seeing him, as we were both avid fans of the brilliant singer.

On Sunday morning, a car picked us up for the drive to Lake Bracciano for the wedding reception of the newlyweds. The home of our hosts, the groom's parents, was an attractive, country house overlooking the lake. The grounds were magnificent, abundant with olive trees and flora of all varieties. Huge rectangular umbrellas were spread out everywhere, covering the tables set all around the pool and on the lawn, creating much-needed shade under the brilliant sun. Champagne and wine were flowing and delicious hors d'oeuvres were served before a sumptuous lunch. About a hundred people were in attendance. A talented young woman played the electric piano; it created a very festive atmosphere. The groom's parents were very warm and gracious and begged us to return to Rome for another visit. It was a beautiful day, a beautiful party and one that remains in my memory.

In the evening, we shared a farewell dinner back in Rome with our dear friends, Joe and Joan, the parents of the bride.

Our trip ended with a wonderful, elated feeling. But I was looking forward to going home, and being with my children. I had so many interesting tales to share with them.

We wander for distraction, but we travel for fulfillment.
    —Hilaire Belloc

For many years, David and I had wanted to visit Ireland. Our New York doctor was Irish and was on the board of the Royal College of Surgeons in Dublin; he promised us a private tour of the facility when we visited Dublin. He also had a relative in Kenmare, who would meet with us. Another Irish friend had a cousin who owned a restaurant in Kenmare. Having personal contacts in a foreign country was always very interesting and helpful. We decided that this was the year for our Irish adventure.

The title of this tale, loosely translated, means "Ireland Forever." It has also been translated as "Ireland until the end of time."

ERIN GO BRAGH

WE LEFT NEWARK AIRPORT for Shannon, Ireland, on August 27th, 1998, arriving early the following morning. The sight of Ireland, as we came close to landing, left me with a very "green" memory. The land is a patchwork quilt of all shades of green farms with houses scattered sparsely on the landscape. The drive from the airport to Cong, our first stop, was about two and a half hours through the beautiful countryside.

We entered the grounds of Ashford Castle through huge park gates open to the public for a fee. Beyond the long drive into the park, we came upon a lush, green golf course, and then the view of Ashford Castle, sitting on the edge of Lough Corrib. We were completely taken back by the view. We thought Chambord, in France, was the largest castle we had ever seen, although it was only a tourist attraction, not a hotel. We had never stayed in a castle or chateau of this proportion.

Everything about Ashford was magnificent. David loved the elegance of our after-dinner coffee and petits fours served in the drawing room, and suggested, *tongue in cheek*, that I should treat him to this kind of service at home.

At around 10:30 p.m., we went down to the Dungeon Bar to listen to the lovely voice of an Irish singer. What a delight! The Irish music was lilting and melodic. We were asked to sing along with some of the melodies. It was a glorious day.

After breakfast the following morning, we drove along the coast road towards Connemara, a wild and beautiful region of mountains, lakes, tumbling streams, undulating bog, sea-girt promontories, unspoiled beaches and panoramic views. Connemara is in Galway County, a Gaelic-speaking region. The mountains, hills, valleys and roads were often dotted with sheep. This was a very "wooly" country. David picked up an Irish accent, and was often taken for a local. He loved languages and enjoyed sounding like the natives.

**Kylemore Abbey, only home to the Benedictine
nuns in Ireland, acquired by the nuns in 1920.**

We travelled throughout the country, stopping to visit many of the famous sites of Ireland, and stayed in castles hundreds of years old, including Dromoland, the sister castle to Ashford. It was difficult to compare the two castles, although the grounds of Ashford, overlooking the lake, I believe were lovelier. But, our room was the most magnificent so far.

Dromoland Castle

We fell in love with the Irish people; they love being hosts and they excel at their job. Everywhere we went we were treated like royal guests. The Irish take great pride in their culinary feats; we feasted like a king and queen, especially when we were guests in these majestic castles.

Before arriving at Dromoland Castle, we drove toward the Cliffs of Moher bordering the Burren, on a tip of land jutting into the North Atlantic—an incredible sight—and climbed towards the top where we were hit with 60 mph winds. The winds stopped us dead in our tracks. The great, dark, sandstone cliffs rose up sheer from the Atlantic for nearly five miles.

After we arrived at Dromoland Castle, the following day, we visited the town of Adare, hoping to have lunch at the well-known Adare Manor. No luck . . . it was closed to the public, due to the impending visit from President Clinton and his entourage. This was not the first time our travels coincided with President Clinton. We seemed to be on the same schedule.

We continued travelling past Killarney, and entered the "Ring of Kerry," a 126-mile road that skirts the Iveragh Peninsula and runs along the coastline between Kenmare in the south and Killorglin in the north. Beautiful landscapes and seascapes could be viewed along the way. David and I loved the long, scenic drives in most of the countries we visited. It gave us time to talk about our lives and some of the problems we all encounter. We often were able to resolve differences, which helped to enhance our travels and kept the romance alive and well.

We arrived in Kenmare in time to shower and dress for dinner at Packies'. The chef, Maura, was the cousin of our friend. Our friend had grown up in Kenmare and was also a friend of the owners of the Park Hotel, where we stayed.

The next day, we visited Maura at her home, Shelburne House, which was also a country lodge and guesthouse. Maura made tea, and we sat and relaxed with her and her husband for a few hours, solving the *problems of the world*. David loved discussing politics and economics. He had Maura and her husband convulsive with laughter. But David's viewpoints were compatible with theirs and the conversation ended amicably. We were even invited back for more "entertainment."

We walked back into town, strolling the charming village, and then headed back to the hotel. We phoned our doctor's cousin, Donal, and asked him to join us for drinks at the hotel. Meeting Donal was a delight. He was the assistant principal and teacher at the local vocational school, and a very warm, charming character. After drinks and chatting awhile, he insisted on taking us for a ride to show us some of the lovely, interesting sights of

Kenmare. Donal then took us to his home to meet his family. His wife insisted that we remain for tea and scones, so we stayed for a while. On the way back to the hotel, Donal drove us to see a beautiful resort, Sheen Falls Lodge, sitting next to a wild salmon lake and river. Watching the salmon jumping was fascinating. It was a gratifying day; the Irish are very warm and gracious people, and very proud of their country.

The Park Hotel, Kenmare

The three days spent in Kenmare were very special, including the brilliant rainbow that arched across the entire village one afternoon after a quick downpour. Rainbows have always held great meaning for me. They bring tears of joy to my eyes, as each time I see one I know blessings are on their way. They have become a good-luck symbol for me.

En route to Dublin we had an overnight stay in Cashel. It was a good interim stop from the west coast, about three hours away from Dublin on the east coast. It was here, in Cashel, where the first Guinness dark beer was brewed in 1759 by Richard Guinness.

We arrived in Dublin the following day at the Hotel Merrion, the newest and most elegant hotel in Dublin. After lunch, we headed to Grafton Street for some shopping. But first, we went through St. Stephan's Park on our way to visit the Royal College of Surgeons. President Clinton had spoken there the day before. Our doctor, who was on the board as chairman of the department of infectious diseases, wanted us to see this famous medical school, which is not open to the public. We were given a private, fascinating tour of the college. It brought back memories of the stories my brother, Mike, would tell me when he went to medical school in Chicago, especially about dissecting the cadavers. My mother always said the wrong one became the doctor, as I was the courageous one and my brother was *squeamish* when we had to bait our fishing hooks with worms; I always had to bait the hooks. I was also fascinated with medicine and would steal my brother's books when he came home from med school, and read them under the covers with a flashlight. But, he became a great doctor.

Dinner that evening was in the hotel, at the number one restaurant in Ireland, Patrick Guilbaud. We made the reservations the week before, as it was difficult to get a reservation. We enjoyed our favorite aperitif, champagne, in the sitting room of the restaurant while ordering our dinner. Champagne was always our favorite drink before dinner, and we followed that tradition for many years at home. David always said that champagne spoke of romance . . . and he was so right. He bought cases of champagne, and I still have the remnants of that collection to this day.

On Sunday we went to the spa and walked on the treadmill. All the marvelous food was beginning to get to us. It was rainy, but after breakfast we braved the nasty weather and returned to Grafton Street and the indoor mall for more shopping. We returned to the hotel to relax for a few hours before dinner and luxuriated in a hot tub. David and I loved taking baths together; that often became some of the fun memories of our travels.

On Monday we left Dublin and flew to Glasgow, Scotland. After arriving in Glasgow, we rented a car and drove directly to Turnberry. We had wanted to play golf at the famous course of Turnberry, and this was our chance.

Turnberry is a small area jutting out into the North Atlantic. The hotel, sitting high on the hill, is a beautiful, imposing structure. The golf course lies across from the hotel, running along the waterfront. We made tee time for 8:00 a.m. the following morning. The winds that evening began whipping up, along with a light rain. During the night the wind and rain *really* picked up.

8:00 a.m., Tuesday morning . . . we were going to play! The winds began to gust, intermittently up to forty miles an hour; but Turnberry is a championship course, and this was our only opportunity. The sky was threatening, but the rains held, except for a few sprinkles on the 18th hole. The sea looked ominous and the course was difficult. Our caddy, Jackie, was terrific; he handed us clubs, suggesting where and what we should hit. David played very well. On the other hand, I did not play as well as I would have liked to. I still recall the incident in the sand trap.

My ball landed in a sand trap with the course about eight feet above my head. I had never seen a sand trap like this . . . *ever*. I swung my club about six times, trying to loft the ball above my head onto the fairway. Jackie stepped forward to pick up my ball, and said, "My lady, we don't let our ladies struggle in the sand traps."

I answered, *"Don't touch that ball. I'm not giving up!"* On the eighth try, the ball flew up and landed on the edge of the grass above my head . . . it was out!

Jackie stepped back in amazement, and said, "You American ladies are very tough."

The experience was great! We walked away exhilarated, and a little lighter in the pocket. Golf was very expensive at Turnberry.

Me playing the course at Turnberry

After leaving Turnberry we drove towards the Highlands, stopping to visit Sterling Castle, the former home to the Stewarts and Mary, Queen of Scots. We had a delightful and humorous, young guide going through the castle. He told wonderful stories and brought the old castle alive with his tales. The kitchen had been completely restored and was very interesting, with wax figures depicting people baking and cooking the food for the castle.

Sterling Castle

Wax figures in the restored kitchen of Sterling Castle

We continued driving to the Highlands, passing through Braemar, where the Gathering of the Clans is held each year. We had just missed it by a week.

David, upon seeing the Scotsmen in skirts, considered buying one, *for fun.* I talked him out of it; although he had gorgeous legs, I couldn't see him wearing a kilt back in the States.

Again, our trip took us through magnificent mountain passes, this time in the Cairngorms. These granite mountains of about three thousand feet appear aubergine as you approach them, and then you realize they are covered in purple heather. The view was dramatic. We finally arrived at our hotel, the Craigendarroch, in the late afternoon. We had a lovely room overlooking the mountains nestled next to the River Dee, where the queen's castle, Balmoral, rests.

In the morning, the next day, we went to the gym before breakfast. Boy! Did we need that after sitting in a car for so many hours a day. After breakfast we headed for Braemar. This beautiful spot is where the river tumbles through a narrow channel, dropping into rocky pools.

In the evening, we relaxed in the living room of our suite watching SKY News on TV. Clinton was all over the screen. I guess we decided to visit Ireland at the same time as the president; he seemed to be one step ahead of us everywhere we went.

Our next accommodations were at Culloden House, just outside of Inverness, in the village of Culloden. Our room was huge, with a comfortable sofa and chairs in front of a working fireplace. The porter started the fire, and we relaxed before dinner with a glass of sherry in front of the fire, while reading and watching TV. *There was Clinton again!* The Irish people loved him.

Culloden House

We dined, on our last evening in Scotland, in the beautiful dining room of Culloden House. After a great night's sleep in our stately bedroom, we awoke to a glorious day for our trip back to Glasgow, and our flight home. We said our goodbyes to Ireland and Scotland. When I look back, I am so grateful that David and I shared this memorable trip.

IN THE SUMMER OF 2000, David and I took our forty-fifth wedding anniversary cruise to Europe. Unbeknownst to us, it was the last voyage David and I would take together. The years of travelling with David were more than fulfilling; they were many of the greatest adventures we shared. I am so grateful for all the wonderful memories that are mine to keep forever.

We attempted to squeeze every bit of joy and pleasure out of the waning years of the twentieth century. The end of a century?!?! Where did a hundred years go? I remember the celebrations and exultation of the year 2000.

I often think of the phrase, *"Man proposes and God disposes."* I'm so glad we had enjoyed those last years of a passing century, for we knew not what was ahead of us in the birth of the twenty-first century. When David passed away in September of 2001, I lost the love of my life . . . my romantic Romeo . . . my favorite travelling companion.

Part Four
IT'S NOT OVER YET YEARS

God leaves the stronger one behind.

The death of a loved one is like a deep wound; it takes time for the healing. An emotional scab forms and eventually, as time passes, drops off. Underneath new emotions grow. Life goes on.

My husband, David, was strong, not only physically, but mentally and emotionally. Throughout his suffering he never complained. But I believe the strength that God gave me held the family together, and gave David comfort in knowing I would be okay.

GOODBYE MY LOVE

IN DECEMBER OF 2000, we moved into the new house we had built in Florida. The move was exhausting, but David was a "trooper." I did most of the packing, but David handled everything else. In between, we managed to do our daily power walk and still, occasionally, enjoy a game of golf to distract us from all the work.

In late January, David was not feeling great. His voice was hoarse, so he visited an ENT specialist. The doctor sent him to a therapist who trained him to speak softly without straining his larynx. He did quite well, although speaking softly for David was not easy; he was used to asserting his strong voice when he wanted things done. Moving into the new house, and dealing with the workmen, was difficult for a man to speak like a lamb when he was really a lion.

March arrived. It was spring break for my grandchildren from Colorado. My son Cliff and his family came to visit in Florida.

A week after they left, my daughter, Tina, was leaving for California to begin chiropractic school. We were very busy helping her pack and shipping furniture for the apartment she would be living in for the next three and a half years. Then we flew with her to San Jose, California. We waited almost the entire week for the moving truck to arrive. Where was it? We were only staying for the week and needed to get her settled, as she was starting school on Monday.

Late Saturday afternoon, the movers arrived. The truck had broken down along the way and was detained three days. This left us with little time to get her unpacked, as we were leaving on Sunday, the following day. We worked through the night, as she would have little time to unpack once school began.

When we arrived back in Florida, David began coughing. It was already April, and we were preparing to leave for our home in Connecticut around May 1st. Although no x-ray was taken, his cough was treated as a chest cold. We still had much work to finish in the new house, and I think David did not want me to know how terrible he was feeling.

The last weekend in April, David was running a fever and had an intestinal upset. When we spoke to the doctor, he said he had the same fever and intestinal problem the week before, and it would pass within a few days. And it did.

When we arrived at our home in Connecticut, in early May, after driving from Florida, David seemed to feel somewhat better. But, a few weeks later the cough began again. Were all these symptoms a sign of what was to come? Was his immune system compromised? We will never know whether any of these illnesses were related to what was discovered in the following weeks.

David's doctor took a chest x-ray. When I viewed the x-ray I was astonished at what I saw; his right lung was a complete fog. He was scheduled for a CAT scan that weekend and the tumor in his right lung was discovered.

He entered the hospital for a lung biopsy the first week in June. There it was---fourth-stage lung cancer. The doctor told me the results after the biopsy was taken, but requested that I wait for him to tell David when we came to his office two days later. David was inoperable.

I could tell no one for two days. I don't know how I slept, ate, moved and breathed for those two days. How could the tumor be fourth stage? David was strong and healthy and he was not a smoker.

David's oncologist was a wonderful doctor and a casual friend. He had been a research oncologist at Stanford University for many years. He was very open-minded when it came to treatments. My family and I began searching for anything new in medicine for David's cancer that wasn't the traditional chemotherapy. We came upon a new protocol in a capsule that was being used for fourth stage lung cancer. It was in trials at Memorial Sloan Kettering Cancer Center in New York City and in Stamford, Connecticut. But, the trials were closed. David's oncologist was a friend of the doctor in Stamford and was able to get David into the trial on "compassionate-use basis." David was so excited and swore he was going to beat this.

Five weeks later, there was no improvement. He continued the therapy for another week, and then had to return the remaining capsules. The cancer had metastasized to his brain and his liver.

David began radiation treatments for the brain cancer. We went to the radiologist each morning for twelve days. Then the chemotherapy began.

I never gave up believing that somewhere, somehow there was a treatment that could save him.

I received information about a Doctor Burzynski in Houston, Texas, who was saving many patients with various cancers. I called and made arrangements to take David to Texas. I hired a Learjet air-ambulance with a doctor and a nurse on board, as David was too ill to fly commercially.

We remained in Texas for two weeks while David was being treated. Monica, my daughter's best friend, and my older son, Cliff, flew with us to Texas. Monica remained with David and me, and Cliff, after a few days, returned to Colorado.

When we arrived we had a consultation with Dr. Burzynski. He told my husband that he could only promise a fifty percent chance of success with his treatment. Although his protocol was saving the lives of children with a type of brain cancer, and many women with breast cancer, each cancer was different. The age of the person and the type and stage of the cancer were all factors. I remember his waiting room, filled with patients, and the walls covered with photos of many famous people, autographed with big "thank yous."

David began his treatment with the capsule version of the protocol. When he reached sixty capsules a day, he could no longer tolerate the treatment. At that point, he was to have a port implanted in his chest, so I could administer the fluid form of his treatment four times a day.

On the morning of September 11th, 2001, we arrived at another doctor's office to have the port implanted. It was 9:00 a.m. in Houston. The doctor was late getting to his office as he was detained at the hospital. The nurses placed David on the operating table and prepared him for the procedure.

A while later, I checked at the front desk to ask when the doctor might arrive. He was already almost an hour late. The nurses were quite upset, saying something terrible had happened in New York City, and sent me to a room with a television. Two planes had hit the World Trade Center in New York City. After the second hit, they knew it was an act of terrorism.

Monica and I took turns staying with David and watching the devastation on television in the other room.

I tried to reach my son, Todd, in New York City, but there was no phone service. I called my son in Colorado. He told me that he heard from

Todd, earlier, and that he had been crying on the phone. Todd's wife was in Chicago on business and could not fly home. Flights were cancelled. His children had left for their school in Riverdale, about a half an hour north of the city. The main arteries leaving New York City were closed. He found a way out of the city and retrieved his children, then drove to his in-laws' on Long Island and remained there for a week. His wife arrived a few days later, after driving to her parents' home on Long Island, from Chicago, with a co-worker.

When I brought David back to the hotel where we were staying in Houston, after the port was implanted, he insisted on watching the news in New York City. He continued to watch the news, day after day. It saddened me deeply to have him so engrossed with the events in New York, for perhaps the last days of his life.

Three days before we were due to return home, David developed pneumonia, and was hospitalized. I pleaded with the doctor to let me take him home. Finally, I made arrangements for another air-ambulance to fly us back to Connecticut. David was taken by ambulance from the plane to our local hospital, where he died a day and a half later.

My daughter flew in from California and arrived after 1:30 a.m. David was in a coma, but they kept him alive until she arrived and was able to say her goodbye.

My son, Todd, and I slept on a pull-down bed in his room. When the nurse came in and told us that it was time, Todd and I sat on either side of his bed and held his hands as he passed away.

Cliff called from Kennedy Airport in New York after arriving from Denver with his family. I told him, "Dad is gone; go directly to the house."

Do you believe in spirits contacting us? I was not a believer . . . but I am now.

Clifford's story is one I shall never forget. When he arrived at the airport in Denver in the wee hours of the morning, he dropped his family at the inside curb before parking the car. The area was deserted at that time of the morning. When Cliff, his wife and two children stepped out of the car, they heard a frantic voice calling, "Cliff . . . Cliff." When they tried to see who was calling his name, no one was there.

They continued to the terminal. Within minutes, a loudspeaker announced, "Paging David Pearl, paging David Pearl." The terminal was almost empty, as the first flights out were about 6:30 a.m., and it was about two hours earlier. Was David calling out to Cliff to say goodbye? I believe he was.

I deeply felt the losses of those lost in the tragedy of 9/11. Somehow, I felt my country and I were in mourning together.

David was buried in Connecticut in September of 2001—he was 69 years old—but in March of 2002, I had him disinterred and reburied in Florida to be nearer to me, since I planned on selling my Connecticut home. Forty people attended the graveside burial in Florida and returned to my home for a party to celebrate his birthday. It was March 18th, David's seventieth birthday.

Note: As of this writing, tomorrow is March 18th. David would have been seventy-nine years old. I continue to celebrate his life.

Widowhood doesn't get better . . . it gets different. Life continues for those left behind, but life still holds many mysteries to be explored. You can discover many joys if you earnestly seek them. Hold on to the three Fs . . . faith, family and friendships.

When my husband David passed away on September 22, 2001, we had married forty-six years. He was my best friend.

The morning of the funeral was cool, with a light rain and a slight wind. My mother would have said, "The heavens are weeping."

Fall had just begun. The leaves started their slow descent to the earth. The colors began to display their beautiful palette, but it was still too early for the transformation. In northern Connecticut, autumn often arrived a little early.

When our entourage arrived at the cemetery, the sun came out and the wind ceased. It was very still. As the last shovel of dirt was thrown into the open grave, one leaf slowly trickled down, landing on the casket. I heard the gasps of everyone, shocked, at the descent of the lonely leaf. There was no wind and there was no tree close to the grave.

The following morning, I awoke very early and went to my small, glassed-in sunroom. I needed to write to my husband. I wrote the following poem; I hope he received it.

THE SENSES OF MY BEING: AN ODE TO MY HUSBAND

I SHALL SEEK YOU IN THE WHISPER of the falling leaves in autumn.

I shall sense you in the gentle snowflakes that trickle down, upon our lake, in winter.

I shall hear you in the raindrops that drench the earth in spring.

I shall see you in the flowers and feel you in the soft breezes of summer.

I will hear your voice in the loving words of our children.

Your laughter will ring in my ears when our grandchildren recall the memories of Grandpa.

I shall know your beauty in the eyes of all who loved you dearly.

I shall feel your touch as you guide me along the way, showing me the paths of knowing and understanding that you tried to teach me.

You remain deep within the earth, but you will always live deep within my heart.

To be depressed is to lose sight of the good that you <u>do</u> have in your life, and to wallow in the negative. It is the lack of what you believe you <u>should</u> have. To be depressed is to be joyless.

FEAR OF DEPRESSION

THE DICTIONARY DESCRIBES DEPRESSION as an emotional condition; gloominess; dejection; sadness; feelings of hopelessness. Being down or having low spirits is usually a sign of depression, but not always. I often say, "I'm not a robot, I'm a human being." But even robots, on occasion, can mechanically default. We as human beings can emotionally default.

Throughout my life, I've had many low periods for multiple reasons, but I never believed I had suffered from depression. It was after losing my husband to a three-and-a-half-month battle with cancer that I was too numb to be depressed. I was burdened with the responsibility of two large homes, 1,250 miles apart. When David died in Connecticut in September, I left for my second home in Florida one month later.

Close friends rallied around me for the six months I remained in Florida. Within that time period, I was only home alone for three evenings. I kept myself busy during those days, and thought I faired quite well. My children lived far away, in three different states: Colorado, California and New York. I visited a psychologist and a psychiatrist and went to two bereavement groups, which I felt weren't helpful. I was more down after the bereavement meetings, listening to everyone's story, than I was before I went. I stopped going after the second meeting. *I thought I could handle it, just fine, by myself.*

I returned to my home in northern Connecticut the end of April, 2002. Living in a large home, fairly secluded, surrounded by woods and sitting on the edge of a lake, was very lonely and sometimes unsettling.

Looking back, I didn't think depression hit me at that time. Perhaps I simply didn't recognize the signs, never having been there before. Like a caterpillar, it crept up slowly. I kept myself as busy as possible with my local friends and drove to New York City on many weekends to be with my younger son, Todd, and his family.

At the end of June, my daughter, Tina, came to stay with me in Connecticut for her three-week break from chiropractic school in California. I planned a fun mother/daughter, three-day stay at a spa in lower

Connecticut for July 4th. It was a mile or so from a popular gambling casino, which we visited a few evenings. I *appeared* to enjoy myself.

Returning home after our excursion, Tina remained with me for the last two weeks of her vacation. I went through all the motions of a loving mother sharing time with her daughter, but I realized something was very wrong. I loved having my daughter with me, but I could feel no joy; I felt dead inside. It hit me like a boulder rolling off a cliff, and I couldn't get out of the way. I said nothing to my daughter, but continued sharing two weeks of busy, fun days and nights.

After Tina returned to California, I went to visit my doctor—a kind, soft-spoken man who had taken care of my husband at the end of his life. He talked to me for a length of time and made me understand that I was in a deep depression, because I was in mourning. It hits people differently and at different times during the mourning period; it can last different lengths of time for each individual. I never saw it coming. He put me on an anti-depressant, which I remained on for about two years. I probably didn't need it for that long; I almost forgot I was taking it along with my vitamins each morning. It was so much a part of my routine.

The second year I returned to Florida, I did a lot of entertaining at home . . . thanking my friends for being there for me. It was another busy season for me and I did quite well emotionally. Was it the medication, my own resilience, or just time, which is a great healer? I truly don't know.

In the pursuing years much happened to lighten the emotionally dead weight. I sold my home in Connecticut in 2003, a huge burden lifted off my shoulders. Tina graduated chiropractic school in June, 2004, and came home to live with me in Florida. I met and had a wonderful relationship with a gentleman in 2004, and I began enjoying travelling again. Life has a way of coming back to square one, but in a different form.

I've had many down periods since then, but I've learned not to fear depression. I know there will be many more lows in my life, but I've learned through reading, sharing with others in special group meetings, learning to value and appreciate all the good in my life, praying and meditating every day, staying close to the people I love and knowing that I have more emotional strength than I ever knew I had. I've come to respect depression for what it taught me about myself.

I have weathered every storm and sailed into calm waters. My faith has carried me through, even as I felt myself drowning in sorrow and self-pity. Coming close to the bottom of a great, steep and dark precipice, I somehow climbed up, struggling with each step, but knowing if I kept going I would reach the warmth of the sun again. I would be okay. I somehow knew my life would steady itself and I would smile and laugh and feel the joy of living again.

To be dead is to be at peace. To feel dead is a living hell.

I no longer fear depression because I know it is only temporary. I know I am the master of my thoughts, my emotions, my life.

Depression doesn't deserve its social stigma; it is an eye-opening phenomenon that can make you a better you. I've come to realize it's a wake-up call to change my thinking.

Webster's dictionary defines "chemistry" as a sympathetic understanding; rapport; sexual attraction. Chemistry is the spark that ignites intimacy. It can't be created in a laboratory. It's a major ingredient in a romantic relationship.

It was Christmas vacation, 2003. Todd and his family were visiting me in Florida for the holidays. I had been widowed for over two years and had started dating through introductions.

My son was sitting at my computer when I entered the room. "Mom," he said, "bring me a photo of yourself. I'm going to put you on this Internet dating site."

I looked at him as if he had two heads. Was he out of his mind? "NO WAY," I answered.

"I'm not leaving here until you fill out this profile and bring me a photo," he insisted.

I finally gave in, without much enthusiasm. He felt my dating life was going nowhere and he was right. *Internet dating might be fun*, I thought.

I didn't know where to begin. What do I say about myself? As a writer, I knew it had to "catch one's eye." It had to be interesting.

I remembered a young woman I knew who had been widowed in her forties. She had told me that she met her second husband on an Internet dating site. What stuck with me was her statement, "Mona, you need to write something outrageous and outstanding." Her new husband told her what caught his attention was not her photo, but her profile.

DATING AND THE INTERNET

IS ROMANCE STILL ALIVE? It must be, since dating websites are so popular. I took the advice of the young woman who achieved a successful relationship, and then marriage, because of the Internet. I was not interested in marriage, but I was not giving up on romance. I had to write a "grabber." And this is what I wrote.

ABOUT ME:

A genetically privileged woman . . . warm and outgoing. I'm 5'6", 128 lbs., dark hair and dark eyes. As a former model, I am not immune to compliments, but at a recent writer's dinner I was flattered when a renowned gentleman said to me, "Do you know you are a Biblical beauty?" I laughed, but when his wife concurred, I was deeply touched. Inner beauty has always taken precedence for me. I am a glass half-full person. Life is a gift and I enjoy it as such. I am widowed, but had a long and wonderful marriage, and am blessed with a great family. I've travelled extensively and continue to enjoy it. I have many passions, including writing, dancing, golf, theater and movies. I spent many years boating, and still love the water. I also enjoy spectator sports. I split my time between NY and FL, enjoying the best of both worlds.

The profile continued and included physical info, lifestyle, background, and personality and interests. Then came the "big ones"—my ideal relationship, my past relationships, what I was looking for, my perfect first date and my ideal match. This was not easy to write.

I wrote the following about my ideal relationship and what I was looking for.

A caring, considerate, fun-loving man with a sense of humor and a zest for life.

Relationships are built on mutual respect and the ability to tune into the other person's feelings, even without the need to express it in words. Chemistry is a major element. Family is very important to me, and I would want that to be as important to him. I could not have a relationship with a bitter person. I would hope he had a happy and rewarding marriage, as I did. It helps to make one seek more of the same. It would be wonderful to meet a man who could share similar experiences to my own life, but differences can make life and relationships very interesting.

PHEW! I FELT A BIT NAKED. I had just *bared* my soul.
Well . . . it worked.

My son was right. Within the first three weeks of signing onto the website, I heard from over seventy men. It became a fun game. I couldn't wait to get home each day to read my newest e-mails. It put a spark back into my dating life.

Some of the responses I received left me tickled, astounded, sometimes sad, and with some good stories to share with my friends. Those, like the ones below, "blew my mind."

A twenty-six-year-old man from New York wrote: "I felt I had to write to you for you are absolutely beautiful and you sound amazing from your profile. I know I may be young in age but I make up for the numbers with experience and spirit. If I have offended you by writing this, please accept my deepest apologies, for that is not my intent. I am a sincere man and I mean what I say and say what I mean."

Another young man, forty-six years old, from Ile-de-France, wrote me a similar e-mail. He was 4'6" . . . a dwarf.

One man, fifty-three years old, was widowed and interested in marriage and hopefully children.

What were these men looking for . . . a mother? I could surely have filled the bill on that one!

Exactly three weeks after this exciting adventure began, I received an e-mail from a very handsome and interesting man. He gave me his telephone number and asked if I would please call him. And I did. We spoke for a while and he wanted to meet me that weekend. I said I would meet with him on Friday, as I had a date on Saturday with a man who had been introduced to me by a friend. I had a date on Sunday with another "e-mail" gentleman who had driven over from the west coast of Florida; I lived on the east coast.

Three men in one weekend! *I could handle this.* Sunday was a no-no; Saturday was a definite no-no. But Friday . . . WOW! The chemistry exploded!

For the next two years and more we became best friends and lovers. The extreme pain of the loss of my husband eased into a dull ache. My life was full again.

Sadly, in March of 2006, he passed away after battling pancreatic cancer for five and a half weeks.

My daughter was ill at the time, and I think in a strange way it kept me sane. My life was completely devoted to my daughter, which left me with little time to grieve.

A year and a half later, a dear friend introduced me to her childhood friend, who was recently widowed. He was a wonderful, fun-loving, caring man who I adored as a good friend. We enjoyed dancing, golf, theater and movies together, but the missing ingredient was chemistry. After ten months we parted as friends.

The following year I decided to try Internet dating again. The first few weeks, once again, were overwhelming. But then, a gentleman e-mailed me who really spiked my interest. We e-mailed back and forth till we finally spoke. I was in New York City for the summer, and he was in Florida. A relationship began to bloom over the phone. In September, I went to visit my daughter, who lived in Florida, and the man and I finally met. The chemistry was alive and well.

Our relationship ended after nine months. Even though we enjoyed each other's company, our lifestyles were too different to make the relationship work.

I've taken a break from dating at this time, as my life is quite full. But, to a single woman who wants to put some "life" back into her life, I would say, "Go for it." I know love and romance are still floating out there, and when I'm ready, I'll reel it in.

My advice is to never give your full name, never give your address, and always meet in a public place, preferably in the daytime, for the first meeting. Talk on the phone, even more than e-mailing. It's much easier to get to know someone after a half-hour chat, than reading a few lines in an e-mail.

There are many ways to find out information about a person. Be wise and use your common sense. I had only good experiences, as did my friends. Trust your instincts, and take it slow. Enjoy!

I wish for every mother the gift of a daughter. My daughter and I are different, yet so much alike. She is my spiritual "buddy" travelling through life.

MOTHER AND DAUGHTER: A JOURNEY OF LOVE

IN MAY, 2004, I flew to Colorado to spend Mother's Day with my son Cliff and his family. My daughter, Tina, called to wish me "Happy Mother's Day" and I mentioned my plan to travel with my friends on a cruise. Tina was graduating chiropractic school in California in June; I would be attending her graduation.

Then I heard, "Mom, can I come with you?" Tina continued to remind me that I had promised to take her on a trip for her graduation present. *You know the answer.*

Tina and I returned home to Florida after graduation, and then flew to New York to join my friends, and together we all caught our flight to Rome. My daughter and I began a beautiful, bonding journey.

We had travelled frequently as a family, and Tina had travelled alone with Mom and Dad on her thirteenth birthday; this was the first time she would travel abroad with just Mom.

We arrived in Rome on a sunny Friday morning in August, and boarded the *Crystal Serenity* for their "Roman Holiday" cruise, departing from Rome/ Civitavecchia, ending in Barcelona, Spain.

We cruised the Mediterranean the following day, which was relaxing for all who had travelled from many areas of the world the day before. Tina had never been on a cruise ship, and was so delighted with all it offered; she loved swimming, lunching and just relaxing poolside.

Mom and Tina—formal night

I smile when I remember her happy face, so calm and peaceful after the pressures of chiropractic school and final exams.

That evening was formal night, and Tina and I donned our dress clothes, put on our makeup, fussing with each other to make our "grand entrance." *It was a great evening!*

Dining each evening, at our assigned table, was very enjoyable. We shared the table with women who were also travelling with their daughters. Tina became friendly with a young woman from California, who was an agent in the movie industry.

In the morning, we arrived in Taormina, Sicily. This was a first for me and Tina; I had never been in Sicily. Taormina is perched on the side of Monte Tauro, and offers a fantastic view of the coast and the Mt. Etna volcano. Tina remembers walking through the black ash spewed from the volcano, and new shoes became the first order of shopping.

Tina was sorry she didn't wear a bathing suit under her clothes, as the beaches below Taormina were perfect for swimming. Returning to the ship, her first activity was to jump in the pool. August is one of the hottest months in Sicily; the pool became a haven, and the ocean breeze was a lifesaver.

Travelling with Tina was very special. Throughout the family's travelling years, Tina and I had never had the opportunity to travel alone, giggling and sharing intimate stories as females do.

We had a casual dinner, and then headed for the gambling casino, where it was *very* cool. Tina is a slots *aficionado*. Later in the evening, Tina decided to enjoy singing in the karaoke lounge; she "wowed" the audience. *Do I sound like a proud mother?* Whenever Tina sings in karaoke clubs, she is often asked if she is professional. Music and singing have always been an important part of her life. When I visited her in California, she took me to a karaoke club where she frequently performed, sometimes singing duets with a male friend. I was blown away.

The following two days, we docked in two ports I had never visited in the Adriatic Sea... Dubrovnik, Croatia and Corfu, Greece. The amazing Old Town of Dubrovnik had many sights, including the well-preserved fifteenth-century walls, which circled the city, and can be walked upon. I was chatting with some of my fellow passengers when I noticed Tina was missing. Minutes later I heard her calling me; I looked up to see her high above me walking on the city walls. I loved it! Tina has always had a fun-loving, childish spirit—I hope she never loses it.

Another formal night . . . Tina, charming the captain

We enjoyed the entertainment that evening, but I was exhausted from the day's activities and left before the show ended, retiring to my cabin. Sitting in the front row, Tina was called up on stage shortly after I left. The zany entertainers, Forever Plaid, asked her to play a song at the piano. They played chopsticks together, and then sang a song together. They gave her a parting gift (dental floss wrapped in a tartan ribbon.) Tina came back to the cabin, laughing hysterically, wishing I had been there to see it. I was sorry I missed her performance.

The next day we arrived in Corfu, Greece, and had a late lunch in a *taverna*. I remembered when the plates were put on the table once before and David threw them onto the dance floor while the music played and the people danced. Tina loved the story about her father and decided to follow his example, throwing the plates and enjoying it. Then she pulled me onto the dance floor and we swayed to the wonderful music.

Sorrento was the next port on our itinerary. Tina had an affinity for Italy since her thirteenth birthday trip; she was happy to be back. Sorrento is also famous for producing limoncello, the aperitif I fell in love with while in Positano. I introduced Tina to this delicious digestif made from lemon rinds.

We boarded a bus in the morning for a five-mile ride from Sorrento to Positano, my favorite place in the world. Tina fell madly in love with Positano. She felt like she'd arrived in heaven, and recently told me she would love to retire there. *Like mother, like daughter.* We stopped at the Hotel San Pietro, where I had stayed with her father.

Returning to the ship, I reflected on a beautiful day, on a beautiful island, and the blessings of having my daughter back in my life after three and a half years in chiropractic school.

We arrived in Florence the following morning, and revisited some of the sites from Tina's thirteen-year-old memory. It had been quite a few years for both of us, returning to this historic and fascinating city. We lunched in a charming, small restaurant off the main square, which I had remembered from years ago. We did more shopping in Florence that day than in any of the ports we had visited. Florence is a great shopping city. Tina could not stop telling me how much this trip meant to her. She was looking forward to returning to Florida with me and living at home till she found her own place. We were so compatible that it was a joy for both of us. She ended up staying with me for three years.

On Sunday, the next day, we awoke in Monte Carlo. Tina and I decided to visit the casino to try our luck. Somehow, again, Tina seemed to be luckier than I was at gambling.

Tina and Mom in front of the Casino in Monte Carlo

Arriving the following day in Portofino was a delight; I wanted Tina to have the pleasure of visiting one of my special places where I had shared so many beautiful memories with her father.

We walked through the tiny streets, browsing in the many boutiques. I took Tina to see the Hotel Splendido, where her father and I stayed; I decided we would lunch on the hotel's terrace restaurant overlooking the water. I loved sharing the experience with my daughter. Returning to the ship in the early afternoon, we relaxed by the pool before dressing for our third formal evening.

Our last port arrived too soon . . . we didn't want this journey to end. We awoke and disembarked in Barcelona the next day, but remained in Barcelona at the Hotel Arts for two nights. The sister of Tina's dearest friend, Monica, lived in Barcelona. We enjoyed a delightful day with her, visiting Gaudi Park. Though this was my third visit to Barcelona in a few years, I had not been to the Park; it was like being in *Alice in Wonderland*. It was surreal. Tina loved Barcelona, and the opportunity to visit Johen, Monica's sister.

This trip has always remained in my heart and memory as a "bonding" story, not a "travelling" story.

Throughout the years, David and I loved travelling with the children, and later, the grandchildren. Tina shared many exciting trips with her brothers and niece and nephews. But, being much younger than her two brothers, when they were in college and later married, as I mentioned earlier, she had the advantage of enjoying adventures alone with her parents. The Club Med in Guadaloupe in 1984, Club Med in Turquoise in 1986 (Todd joined us), and Club Med in St. Moritz, Switzerland in January 1990, were among her favorites.

Tina and Dad—St. Moritz, 1990

In January, 2011, Tina and I took another "bonding" trip. We took the *Holland America's Westerdam* to the Caribbean for a Hay House seminar cruise, with speakers Dr. Wayne Dyer, Dr. Brian Weiss, Cheryl Richardson, Caroline Myss, John Holland, and many others. We shared a great spiritual journey.

Travel, in the younger sort, is a part of education; in the elder, a part of experience.
—Francis Bacon

TRAVELLING ALONE: 2005

IN 2005, I SOLD my home in Delray Beach, Florida, and moved into an apartment in a much larger resort community in Boca Raton, Florida; I no longer wanted the responsibility of a house. My brother suggested that I buy an apartment in the resort community in which he owned a home. It was a better choice for me, as there were also hundreds of single people, compared to fewer than fifty singles where I was living. It was, literally, a great move.

I had seven weeks to renovate, paint and move into my new apartment, before I left for New York City on my way to Paris, connecting to Nice on the French Riviera. I needed to get away.

Arriving in Nice, I taxied to Monte Carlo to board the *Seabourn Legend* on a cruise to the Cote D'Azur and the Spanish Isles. I sucked in my stomach, took some deep breaths, and told myself, *"I can do this."* I was a bit edgy; I had never travelled abroad alone.

When I boarded the ship, I was given a warm and gracious welcome by one of the ship's officers. I remember his words as he placed his arm around my shoulders: "We take care of our single ladies." And they did.

From that point on, I rarely felt alone; I felt at home. The *Seabourn* ships are small, carrying a capacity of about 215 passengers. Returning to my cabin, each afternoon, I found an invitation on my bed inviting me to dinner with the captain (twice), the engineer, the ship's doctor, the director of entertainment, etc. I began to politely refuse some of the invitations as time went on, as two lovely couples took me *under their wings,* and insisted that I dine with them. I felt very comfortable and began to relax and enjoy myself.

The Adonomises, me, and the Peterses, my new friends

We sailed from Monte Carlo at 6:00 p.m. that evening and arrived in Le Lavandou, France, early the following morning. I boarded a bus that took us through the Massif des Maures, along a hairpin road that afforded a breathtaking view of the indented coastline, covered with beautiful mimosa, palm and gum trees. We continued to an ancient village, Bormes Les Mimosas, renowned as one of France's most attractive and flower-filled villages. The fabulous panoramas and the brilliant flowers drew many artists, painters and sculptors to the village. I longed for David to be with me to enjoy the magnificent views. We had loved the coastline of France and had shared this experience many times before. Now my memories blended with the wonderful sight I viewed on my own.

In the evening, I dined with Captain Thue-Nilsen, *a very handsome gentleman.*

Our next port the following morning was Cannes where I went topless in 1975 and *never again!* My newfound friends and I decided not to take a tour, as we all knew Cannes from years before. We wandered around this beautiful seaport town, enjoying lunch and shopping.

Upon returning to the ship, that evening I dined with the ship's doctor, a charming man. At around 10:00 p.m., there was music and dancing "Under the Stars," then an hour later, we were treated to a "Sail-Away Party."

On Wednesday, the next day, we cruised the Mediterranean. I loved coming down for breakfast each morning, when I was greeted by the waiters. "Good morning, Mrs. Pearl. Did you sleep well last night? How are you on this fine day? May I carry your tray to a table? Where would you like to sit?" What a delight! I kept reminding myself, *You're on your own, Mona.* But being on a small ship, I realized, was a great choice for my first time travelling alone.

Thursday morning we arrived in Mahon, Menorca in the Balearic Islands, and proceeded to Sant Patrici, to visit a local cheese factory. *Delicious!* The highlight of the day came next. In Son Martorellet we watched an exciting performance of the skilled "dancing" Menorcan horses. They

were amazing! I had always loved horses, as I rode as a young girl and later belonged to a riding club, and often rode at dude ranches.

Son Martorellet—
the Menorcan horses

207

At night, we delighted in a great barbecue, on deck, under the stars, then we were entertained by a group of dancers performing the dance music of the 50s, 60s, 70s, and 80s and beyond. My new friends and I decided to try our own dancing skills after the show was over; the music was so contagious. We all danced together; I never felt like the fifth wheel. I have found that people are often very generous in embracing a single woman alone when the woman is open and friendly. I always had the good fortune to attract people by my outgoing nature.

We remained in the Balearic Islands the following morning, arriving in Palma de Mallorca. I had always wanted to visit Mallorca, and I was happy I finally had the opportunity. There was something inspirational about this place; its temperate climate and its beauty had drawn many artists and poets, including Joan Miro, who was born in Mallorca.

We returned to the ship for a glorious evening. The menu for dinner was outstanding, as were all the dinners on the ship. We dined on Alaskan king crab, glazed scallops, roast rib of lamb, and the chocolate piano surprise for dessert. After dinner, the entertainment for the evening was called "Showtime—Broadway in Concert." Every evening was spectacular. *What a way to live!* I loved returning to places I had visited with David and seeing new places for the first time, but even more, I loved our days at sea, talking to people I had just met. The people on board were so warm and friendly that sometimes I forgot I was travelling alone.

I awoke the following morning as we docked in Valencia and was told there would be a surprise awaiting us. We arrived at a jewel in one of the most idyllic settings—the Santa Maria Monastery at El Puig. The motor coach delivered us to the front steps of the cloister, where curators led us through a maze of rooms, including the chapel, the royal drawing room and refectory. Arriving in the refectory, we were greeted with our surprise: We were being entertained by a concert of classical musicians. We were served drinks and canapés before the concert; what an experience in that beautiful setting.

In the evening, after dinner, we enjoyed a "Movie Under the Stars." I had not seen the movie *Hitch* with Will Smith; it felt like the drive-in movies at home, but much more luxurious; relaxing in the evening air at sea was *wonderful.*

On Sunday morning we docked in Barcelona, ending the first leg of the cruise. Many people left and others boarded the ship for the second leg of the journey. Since I had been in Barcelona the year before with my daughter, I decided to sleep late and enjoy a restful day on the ship. I took a long walk along the pier where the boat was docked and discovered a tented flea market at the end of it. I found some great buys and had fun for a few hours. I had become so comfortable as a single woman on board that I was delighted that I had booked my trip for the two-week cruise. I didn't want to leave after the first week, and was looking forward to meeting new people.

We remained docked overnight in Barcelona, and then sailed for Palamos, Spain early the following morning. There were new people to meet at breakfast that morning, including a group of five single friends travelling together. I enjoyed sharing time with them on this second leg of my journey; they came from different parts of the USA, and were very friendly and lots of fun. They asked me to join them on the trip into Girona, an hour drive west of Palamos. Girona is known as the "immortal city" of Spain; it's rich in historic treasures. We walked through one of the best-preserved Jewish communities, inhabited for almost seven centuries.

Returning to the ship for the evening, I had the second invitation to dine with the captain. I couldn't refuse! Before dinner everyone aboard enjoyed the "Captain's Gala Cocktail Reception." The main course for dinner was a *tough* choice! As stated on the menu: lobster, lobster, lobster (lobster tail, lobster spring roll, lobster salad and lobster sauce) or filet of beef Wellington. My daughter, the lobster maven, would have been in *seventh heaven.*

Goodbye Spain, hello France. We awoke the following morning in Port-Vendres, France. Our tour took us to Collioure, where the Pyrenees Mountains meet the Mediterranean Sea. The charming village of Collioure is beautifully situated between two small ports. Here a trio of sheltered beaches line the harbor with the massive royal castle above. The brightly painted houses in contrast to the mountains attracted artists to Collioure for centuries. Matisse, Picasso, and Dali all fell in love with Collioure.

The church in the Port d'Amont on the sea in Collioure

The beach in Collioure, dominated by the royal castle above

Our exclusive event of the day took place at the stately Palace of the Kings of Mallorca, the royal residence to the kings of Mallorca and Aragon during the thirteenth and fourteenth centuries. A great treat was in store; a private reception with cocktails and canapés was held in the King's apartment. Then a Catalan group, dressed in local costume, performed a selection of folkloric songs for our pleasure.

The Catalan singers wishing me a farewell

Music and a yummy fruit flambé, on the deck, "Under the Stars," ended a perfect day. I was too tired to enjoy the show that evening, and retired to my cabin earlier than usual. Every evening was a happening on deck, "Under the Stars," and the clear nights and star-filled skies created a beautiful ending to the delightful and exciting days.

Throughout my voyage I kept thinking how my life had changed in the four years that David had been gone. I was still able to enjoy so much that life had to offer. I had a wonderful family that I adored, great friends, my health and the resources to live a very fulfilling life. I knew how blessed I was, but I also knew it was up to me to open my heart and mind to accept the changes and never feel sorry for myself. *Look where I was and what I was doing!*

The next port on this incredible journey was Marseille, France's second city and home to the Mediterranean's largest port. Classic French cafes and restaurants nestled around gently bobbing fishing boats in the harbor. We visited all the important sites of the city, when free time was afforded, and then I explored the city's quaint areas with my new friends. After four hours, we were happy to return to the ship for another wonderful and relaxing barbecue "Under the Stars."

On to Sanary-sur-Mer the following morning, a tiny gem set in the coast's richest wine region, in the quaint village of Le Castellet; we walked its old, tiny streets where craftsmen and restaurateurs extended a friendly welcome. A short scenic drive then took us to Domaine de Souviou to explore the vineyards and taste the local wine. The return trip to the boat was very quiet. Everyone on the bus fell asleep. After dinner, I decided to try my luck at the gambling casino. *No luck.* My talents are better used elsewhere.

On the following day we arrived at our last stop, St. Tropez, where memories of my visit with David, in 2000, came flooding back. Strolling the streets of St. Tropez, David had spotted a beautiful, painted sleigh bed in the window of a furniture store. We were to move into our newly built home in Boca Raton that December. David decided it was the perfect bed for the guest room, which would be Tina's room when she came home. We ordered the bed. It took six months to arrive and it was perfect for the room. The bed now belongs to Tina, where she enjoys it in her own home today.

Our last evening "Under the Stars" we watched the movie, *In Good Company,* with Dennis Quaid and Scarlett Johansson. After the movie, I sat with my new friends, chatting for another hour before retiring. The ship was due to arrive in Monte Carlo at 7:00 a.m. The guests were heading to the airport in Nice for their trip home to many areas of the globe. My flight took me back to Paris, where I had to stay overnight at the airport and connect with my flight to New York the following morning.

When I travelled alone on this small ship, a degree of camaraderie formed. This became a great advantage, as I never felt alone. I met and got to know many people, and many got to know me; that was the best part of the experience. I learned I could do anything I set my mind to, with strength and confidence.

"We'll never know" . . . a phrase we have all used when circumstances, sometimes, evolve in ways that seem to have no logical reason. God works in mysterious ways.

In the summer of 2001, while researching every avenue available to help my husband survive lung cancer, I called a small nutritional supplement company I knew. I asked if a particular supplement might be helpful for my husband. The receptionist transferred my call to their oncology nurse.

An oncology nurse . . . with a supplement company? I didn't know that existed.

The nurse spoke to me for a while. She was very kind and said she was sending me a book as a gift. A few days later, *The Alpha Lipoic Acid Breakthrough* arrived. The author, Dr. Burton Berkson, had saved the lives of many people from liver failure.

I took the book to my husband's oncologist, who called Dr. Berkson to ask if his procedure would be of help to my husband, as the cancer had metastasized to his liver.

Both doctors agreed it was not for my husband. But, Dr. Berkson recommended taking my husband to Dr. Burzynski in Houston, Texas. I took his advice and flew my husband to Houston. Unfortunately, it was too late for my husband, but five years later, it was not too late for my daughter.

The simple act of making a telephone call to a supplement company, I believe saved her from a possible liver transplant, if not worse. Had my husband not been so ill, I would never have made that phone call. I would never have known about Dr. Berkson. To this day, in a strange way, I believe this was my husband's gift to the daughter he loved.

A GIFT FROM HER FATHER

MY DAUGHTER, TINA, came to live with me in Florida after graduating from chiropractic school in California. After practicing in Florida for a year and a half, she decided to move to New York, and take the boards for New York and New Jersey.

It was December of 2005. Since I had an apartment in New York City, we decided to spend the Christmas holidays in the big city. Tina could then remain in my apartment indefinitely, while she pursued her career, when I returned to my home in Florida.

She had a busy January in the city, getting in touch with old friends and making new contacts to help her establish a practice in New York.

At the end of January, 2006, she picked up a parasite, and was treated. The treatment did not go too well, and within less than two weeks she developed flu symptoms. She was then put on another drug. I believe this was the final blow.

As usual, Tina tried to spare her mother the details of her illness. She knew I was flying to Philadelphia that Monday, February 13th, to be with a very close friend, dying of cancer, at the University of Pennsylvania Hospital.

PHASE I

Sunday morning, February 12th, 2006, the Blizzard of '06 hit New York City with a fury. Central Park recorded 26.9 inches of snow, which beat the previous record of 26.4 in December, 1947. No aboveground transportation in the city was available, and most flights out of local airports were cancelled.

Relaxing with my first cup of coffee that Sunday morning in sunny Florida, I wasn't aware of the major storm in New York. When I turned on the TV, I was amazed to see what was happening in the city. I decided to wait awhile to check on Tina, since she loved sleeping late on Sundays, and she wasn't going anywhere in this storm. I believed she was feeling much better since we spoke yesterday.

Shortly after, the phone rang. Tina's weak and weary voice was on the other end. "Mom, I woke up this morning and looked in the mirror. My face is blown up and I look like a chipmunk and I'm having a hard time breathing."

"Call your brother, Todd, and let him take you to a hospital . . . IMMEDIATELY," I shouted. My son, Todd, lived a block away from my apartment in the city.

The nearest hospital by subway was Lenox Hill Hospital on 77th St. and Park Avenue. The closest hospital by foot was New York Presbyterian Hospital on York Ave. and 68th Street. But, Tina could never have walked the distance. It was only a short walk to the subway.

Todd responded quickly, and got her to the hospital. She spent a few hours in the emergency room after they gave her shots of prednisone.

Todd called me from the hospital to update me, and told me not to worry. Things were under control. Hours later, when Tina finally arrived home, she called to tell me she was breathing much better and now she only looked like the baby chipmunk instead of the mommy.

I called every few hours to check on her, and she seemed to be doing much better. I thought, *Thank God, Tina's going to be OK.*

The following morning I left for Philadelphia to visit my hospitalized friend. I returned to Florida after three days at the hospital, constantly checking in with Tina.

I was home only a day when I received a call from Tina that her doctor was checking her into the hospital. She had become jaundiced.

I flew to New York City on the next flight. Tina was in Lenox Hill Hospital when I arrived. I was in shock when I saw her. She was the color of amber, and was hooked up intravenously. They were taking extensive tests to determine the cause of her illness. She was in good hands, under the care of the chief of gastroenterology.

After nine days in the hospital it was determined she had cholestatic hepatitis and pancreatitis. Her liver was not functioning properly. But, the answer to the original question of the cause of the illness was still uncertain.

After Tina was released from the hospital, we visited the doctor every few days for blood tests.

Tina's color continued to worsen and she was scratching her whole body as the condition caused severe itching. Her body became covered with scabs, and she was losing weight.

I remained in New York taking care of my daughter while she was supposedly recuperating. Norman Cousins had written that humor was an excellent way to help heal the body. We brought in as many humorous DVDs as we could find, including the old slapstick comedies and *Wallace & Gromit*. We enjoyed watching them together, and really laughed heartily.

Tina's spirit always remained positive and I prayed she was on her way to recovery.

More than two and a half weeks after Tina's release from the hospital, on Friday, March 17th, I received a call that my dear friend had died. On Sunday, March 19th, my son, Todd, said he was going to drive me to Philadelphia to attend the funeral. He knew how much this wonderful man meant to me.

I was concerned about Tina being alone, but she insisted she could manage just fine for the day.

A few days later, we had another meeting with the doctor. He took us into a conference room and told us he needed to discuss the next step with us. He wanted Tina to meet with a team of liver transplant surgeons.

The words hit me like a sledgehammer. All I could think was, *I'm out of here!* I thanked him and said we would consider it. I then took Tina back to the apartment.

The title of Dr. Berkson's book kept jumping into my head. *Where was that book?* Having two homes, I had my library of books split between both places.

Returning to the apartment, I opened the door to the cabinet that held my books. *The Alpha Lipoic Acid Breakthrough* was staring at me. I read the book for the second time.

The following morning, I called New Mexico, where Dr. Berkson practices. The receptionist switched me to the office manager, Dr. Berkson's wife. She was very kind and listened to my story of Tina. I asked when I could bring Tina to see Dr. Berkson. She hesitated, then said he could see her in six weeks.

I was devastated and tried to hold back the tears. I pleaded my case and said, "You don't understand. Her doctor is considering a liver transplant. My daughter may be dying."

There was a moment of silence then she asked, "How soon could you bring her here?"

"Tomorrow," I replied.

My next phone call was to make flight arrangements to El Paso, Texas, then arrange for a rental car to drive the forty-two miles to Las Cruces, New Mexico, to Dr. Berkson's office.

I also made arrangements for the inn where we would live, close to the doctor's office, for the next eleven days.

The following day we left for New Mexico. I ordered wheel chair service at the airport, as Tina could only walk short distances. She was very weak and frail, and had lost twenty-seven pounds. She was a shell of the daughter I knew and loved.

When it was time to board the plane, they took us in an elevator down to the tarmac and wheeled her to the plane. She was then assisted up the steps onto the plane.

We were on our way, and for the first time since Tina had become so ill, my heart felt like a phoenix rising. I knew this wonderful doctor was going to make her well.

PHASE II

The trip went well, although it was exhausting for Tina. We settled into the suite of the inn we would be living in for the next eleven days, minutes from

Dr. Berkson's office.

Tina's first examination was extensive. Dr. Berkson used both conventional and alternative methods of treatment. I was impressed with the entire program. The clinic was set up in a large room to accommodate perhaps eight people at one time. Large lounge chairs circled the room, and next to each one was the familiar pole to hang the intravenous solution that most patients would be hooked up to, twice a day. It reminded me of a chemotherapy room, which I had seen too often. But fortunately, unlike chemotherapy, this was a natural solution of vitamins and supplements to support the immune system, and was individualized for each patient.

Dr. Berkson was very warm and friendly as was his staff. He instilled a strong sense of confidence in both Tina and me.

The treatment began each morning. Tina relaxed in one of the lounge chairs while she received her IV. The solution was amazing. It included alpha lipoic acid and much more; I didn't know the formula, but it seemed to work miracles for so many.

I sat with Tina during her treatments enjoying the company of the other patients, each sharing their own experiences. The office workers made every effort to create a pleasant environment, and they succeeded. There were people from all over the United States, and, I understand, there were also people who came from other countries.

Each day, we listened to the stories of those who shared the treatment room. I remember the pharmaceutical executive who was being treated and had previously brought his wife to Dr. Berkson. She was not being treated at the time, but he told us his wife had been successfully treated at the clinic.

Another gentleman was a doctor, who had been a recreational drug user in the 60s. He developed cirrhosis of the liver, and came to the clinic a few times a year for treatment; he was living a normal, healthy life.

One woman was undergoing chelation for heart disease, and another woman was taking a treatment for pancreatic cancer. The stories each day gave Tina and me the feeling that we were in the right place.

Each afternoon, Tina returned for a second treatment. But, early afternoons, Dr. Berkson wanted her exposed to the brilliant New Mexico sun, for at least twenty minutes a day. I think it was then that I first realized the therapeutic value of the sun to heal. Instead of turning darker, Tina was turning a little lighter each day.

I enticed Tina with every tempting food I could find, including dinners at a small cafe across from the doctor's office. I hoped to add a few pounds to her skeleton frame.

When time permitted, I took her to the movies to see Steve Martin, playing the role of Inspector Clouseau in *The Pink Panther*. That movie was great medicine for Tina and for me, too!

After eleven days of treatment, I flew Tina back to my home in Florida. For another full year she was to continue to take low-dose naltrexone, made by a compounding pharmacist, as well as a protocol of vitamin supplements prescribed by Dr. Berkson. There were monthly "office visits" with Dr. Berkson, by phone, to chart her progress. Her blood work was done every two weeks and forwarded to the doctor.

The recuperation was slow, but steady. Tina lost almost a year of her working life as a chiropractor.

When she began working again, she made the decision to remain in Florida.

One year after she had returned to Florida, she had her last phone consultation with Dr. Berkson. I remember her telling me his last statement: "Tina, now I can tell you. You were a very sick girl."

Today, Tina is a flourishing, healthy young woman, enjoying the fruits of her career she worked so hard to achieve.

There is a blown-up photo of Tina's smiling face on the wall above my computer desk. When I work at the desk, I look at that picture and cannot help but smile back. Her eyes are telling me, "It's OKAY MOM . . . I'm fine."

I have found out that there ain't no surer way to find out whether you like people or hate them than to travel with them.
   —Mark Twain

Phyllis and I have been friends for more than thirty years. After we were both widowed, we became closer friends; today we are inseparable friends. We laugh together, cry together, bitch and complain together; we know each other's moods by the tone in our voices and the look on our faces. Mark Twain was right. When we began travelling together in 2006, we discovered how much we <u>liked</u> each other. Or perhaps love is a better word.

FOREVER FRIENDS: TRAVELLING THROUGH LIFE

MY FIRST TRIP ABROAD WITH PHYLLIS was on a river boat cruise on the Rhine and the Moselle in Germany, on the *Avalon Tapestry*. Neither of us had ever been on a river cruise and we found it very interesting and relaxing on this "floating home." While remaining close to shore, we could observe the towns and villages on both sides of the river.

Before we sailed for Dordrecht in the evening, we were taken on a sightseeing canal boat cruise in Amsterdam, arranged by the *Tapestry*. Canal boats are the best way to see Amsterdam. David and I had been to Amsterdam twenty-three years earlier and I enjoyed sharing the sights of Amsterdam with Phyllis on my return to this charming city. I told Phyllis about our visit to the Anne Frank House. When I visited this historic site for the second time, it was comforting to have her share this experience with me as, at a certain point, David had been unable to continue the tour of the house. He was too emotionally moved. I think it hit Phyllis and me the same way on my second visit, but we completed the tour of the house.

Arriving in Dordrecht the next morning, (I must mention how smooth the sailing is on a river boat compared to a cruise ship; I slept like a baby) we boarded a bus, which took us on a trip to Kinderdijk to see windmills, windmills, windmills. Returning to our boat, we then departed for Rotterdam.

After a two-hour trip, we arrived in Rotterdam; a bus was awaiting us for a visit to The Hague, the seat of the Dutch Government. It is an International Criminal Court, a permanent tribunal to prosecute individuals for crimes against humanity, genocide, war crimes and others. It's a fascinating place.

Our river cruise took us to many cities, towns and villages along the way, some more interesting and memorable than others.

Evenings on the boat were relaxing and delightful, as the days were full with touring. Each night, two movies were offered; Phyllis and I are movie buffs, and caught up with all the movies we had missed and repeated a few. Small local groups from the ports we docked in for the evening provided entertainment. Our cruise director, Hendrik Jan, was a gentleman from Amsterdam. He often spoke after dinner, and told us so much about Germany. One of his talks has remained with both Phyllis and me to this day.

He told us that for many years, the Holocaust was not taught by the schools in Germany. When the present generation became aware of this, they forced the educational system to teach the Holocaust in the schools. I will admit, we both were somewhat apprehensive about visiting Germany, but we found ourselves very comfortable. The German people were very warm and have an excellent relationship with the United States.

We visited Arnhem, known for being one of the biggest Allied tragedies in WWII history, and then continued sailing to Cologne, which was in a frenzied state at the time we arrived. The World Cup was being held in Germany in twelve cities; the match between Togo and France was to be played the next day in Cologne, and the young people were dancing in the streets. Lunching at an outdoor cafe, we could barely hear ourselves, as the people were shouting and singing. The atmosphere was very festive and catching; we found ourselves joining in.

We departed Cologne in the evening, and arrived the following morning in Coblenz, where the Rhine and the Moselle come together. We headed for the Mittelrhein Museum, which was exhibiting works of Salvador Dalí.

Phyllis and I shared much of our time together in Florida in the winter, in

Thumbs up for Phyllis and me in the garden of the museum

the Boston area in the summer with her family, and in New York City at my apartment, but we had never spent entire days travelling together. We discovered how compatible we were and our old, tried-and-true friendship blossomed into an even more meaningful relationship. We knew we would continue to travel together for many years to come.

We left Coblenz and sailed up the Moselle River, reaching Cochem about five hours later. Our tour in Cochem involved visiting the Reichsburg (castle), towering on a mighty rock above the town of Cochem, and afterwards we walked through the colorful town. Though we spent only about three hours in Cochem, it was a photographer's dream. Recently, Phyllis reviewed some of the photos for my book and felt the excitement of the trip return. Our views of Germany changed from the onset of our voyage to the very end of the trip. We both realized that one cannot judge today's generation for the actions of those that came before. (Sin of the Fathers, Exodus 20:5)

The town of Cochem on the left bank of the Moselle

The Reichsburg Castle on the hill above Cochem

View from Cochem across the river to the vineyards above Assmanshausen

Phyllis and me, "friends forever" resting in the shade in Cochem

Trier, the oldest city in Germany, built by the Romans, was the next stop along the river.

Strolling the garden of the Electoral Palace in Trier

That afternoon, we boarded a motor coach for Luxembourg, a land-locked country bordered by Belgium, France and Germany—the world's only remaining sovereign grand duchy. It's one of the smallest countries in Europe but the world's second largest investment fund center after the United States.

We continued by bus to Bernkastel, and visited a wine museum for a wine tasting while waiting for our boat, the *Tapestry*, to arrive. The wine was a little *too good*; most of us slept our way back to meet the boat. Phyllis and I are not afternoon drinkers.

Returning to the Rhine River, we reached Rüdensheim, a winemaking town. It's part of the UNESCO World Heritage Site, located in the Rhine Gorge. We boarded a little tourist train to Siegfried's

A beautiful bend on the Moselle River

Mechanical Music Cabinet Museum,[1] which houses one of the largest collections of self-playing musical instruments in Germany. This fascinating collection encompasses a great range of varied instruments, from a delicate musical watch to the only example of a Poppers Violinovo which is a piano, percussion and a single violin with one bow that bounces back and forth between two playing strings. Phyllis and I both loved the museum; we saw the most novel instruments that we had ever seen or heard. That night we enjoyed a delightful musical evening onboard. Not with the instruments we saw that day!

Mainz was our next stop and included a visit to the Gutenberg Museum, one of the oldest museums of printing in the world; the Gutenberg Bible is on view there.

In the afternoon we boarded a coach for a trip to the city of Worms, which has existed since before Roman times. The Reformation began in Germany in 1517 when Dr. Martin Luther attended the Imperial Diet of Worms.

In contrast, we visited the old Jewish cemetery. Today the Rashi House is the site of the city archives, and the Jewish Museum, documenting the history of the Jewish community of Worms. Between the year 1000 and the darkness of the Nazi regime, a Jewish community had been thriving in Worms. In more recent years a population of Russian Jews has come to live in Worms.

The city was nearly destroyed twice in its history: in 1689, by French troops during the War of the Palatine Succession, and again, it was heavily bombed in 1945 by the Royal Air Force during the last few months of World War II.

Phyllis and I talked a lot about the impact of the Nazi era in Germany. It was evident in so many places we visited along the way, especially in Speyer, the next city on the cruise.

Resting on a Memorial

Speyer has an interesting history, taking it back to about the year 150 AD, when it appeared on the Greeks' world map under a different name.

Speyer was a center for Jewish scholarship in the medieval period. In 1933, as the Nazis seized power, the eight-hundred-year Jewish history in Speyer was brought to an end with the burning of the synagogue in November, 1938. The Jewish "ritual bath" remains and is one of the most complete in Europe, along with the ruins of the synagogue.

After lunch we departed for another coach ride to Heidelberg, where we would visit the famous castle. Heidelberg also boasts the oldest university in Germany. We both did not expect so many side trips on buses along the way, but it afforded a greater overview of Germany outside of the major cities like Berlin and Munich.

Heidelberg Castle hovering over the city

We enjoyed a hilarious evening aboard ship; we were entertained by a "Crew Show." Evenings on a riverboat are very different from those on a cruise ship. The size of the riverboat allows for small, intimate performances, which are often a lot of fun. Where Phyllis and I live in Florida, we love going to comedy shows throughout the winter.

Our riverboat headed for Kehl that evening. Upon arrival, we were taken by coach to Strasbourg, the capital and principal city of the Alsace region of northeastern France. Even though it is a French city, there is still a strong cultural influence from Germany. The mixture of the two countries is present in the local cuisine.

After lunch we departed again by coach for the Alsace Countryside. We had a delightful afternoon leisurely driving through the picturesque countryside with a stop at one of their famous wine cellars for a wine tasting, and then visited Ribeauville, a typical Alsace town. The wine did its job again. Phyllis and I took a long *snooze* all the way back to our boat, resting up for the Captain's "Farewell" dinner.

In the morning we arrived in Breisach, Germany, located at the foot of Kaiserstuhl Mountain on the French-German border. Breisach is the gateway to Germany's Black Forest region, an area of unrivalled beauty with its forests of thick pine trees. And of course, we stopped for "Black Forest" cherry cake. *Yummm!*

We lunched aboard our ship, and then we took a tour to Colmar, known as the birthplace of the Statue of Liberty. We felt as if we were in the middle of a fairy tale, walking though the beautiful town of Colmar, with its famous timber-framed houses, second to none in the world.

At happy hour that evening, we were handed a farewell drink upon entering the lounge, then proceeded to watch the movie *Mona Lisa Smile* after dinner. We talked a lot that evening about our next voyage. We loved the trip but decided that once was enough for a riverboat cruise. This was also the most educational trip that Phyllis or I had ever been on, but it was fascinating, and we learned so much about the history of Germany.

We sailed for Basel, Switzerland, that evening, the last night of our cruise, arriving in the morning for our transfer to Zurich and our return flight home. At the end of the cruise Phyllis and I did not have to say goodbye to one another for long. I returned to New York; Phyllis returned to Boston, to her daughter's home for the summer, and I went to Boston to spend the following week with her. We loved travelling together, and knew we would be doing it again in the near future. And we did.

In June of 2007, Phyllis and I embarked on our next adventure, travelling to Eastern Europe with three couples who were close friends of Phyllis. The itinerary included Vienna, Budapest, Krakow, Warsaw, Berlin and Prague; we were treated to the highlights of all these fabulous cities.

In Budapest we followed the Danube Valley and viewed the ornate Parliament across the Danube River, then delighted in an evening of Hungarian music and cuisine.

The Parliament of Budapest along the Danube River

Travelling into Slovakia through the Tata Mountains, we arrived in Krakow. Krakow has remained with Phyllis and me as the most memorable visit of our trip.

First was the seven-centuries-old Wieliczka Salt Mine on the outskirts of Krakow, where we took a wooden stairway 378 steps down sixty-four meters to a subterranean world of chambers filled with absolutely unique scenes and figures sculpted of salt by the miners themselves. We entered a huge hall, lit with crystal chandeliers fashioned out of the rock salt. We toured the largest underground chapel in a subterranean church carved in

One of the crystal chandeliers made of rock salt rock salt, while continuing to the depth of 135 meters, through the corridors, viewing the statues and lakes. An elevator took us back up the 135 meters to the surface. In 1978, the salt mines were placed on the UNESCO list of the World Heritage Sites.[2] To Phyllis and me, this belonged with the Seven Wonders of the World.

The second visit was heart-wrenching and somber. We toured the Auschwitz concentration camp and nearby Birkenau. At the entrance to the camp is the infamous sign in German that states "Arbeit Macht Frei" ("Work makes one free"). Auschwitz was the largest of the Nazi death camps, where 1.1 million people were murdered. After our visit to Auschwitz, Phyllis and I went across the road to Birkenau and walked the railroad tracks on which the freight cars brought the people to their death. We both cried.

The entrance to Auschwitz: "Arbeit Macht Frei"

Fortunately, that evening we were treated to a Polish dinner and a local folklore show with a live band, and were entertained with songs and dances during dinner. We desperately needed something to lift our spirits; the evening really helped. I shared with Phyllis some of the following stories of those who were close to me, who lived through the Holocaust.

The memory of a dear old friend who committed suicide in her later years because she could not rid herself of the childhood memories from the Holocaust has always haunted me.

Walking the tracks in Birkenau, I recalled the story of my husband's former business partner, who had lost his entire family in the camps, but had been kept alive at the age of sixteen because he was strong and forced labor was needed in the camps. His job was to walk through the pits of dead bodies and remove the gold teeth from the corpses.

I remembered one of my mother's dearest friends. As a young child I often asked my mother why my Aunt Tillie had numbers on her arm.

It was difficult to let go of my feelings towards the people of Poland, but, as I have mentioned before, we found the people to be warm and welcoming and Phyllis and I were determined to accept today's generation and not hold them responsible for their ancestors.

We travelled the following day to Warsaw, visiting the Wilanów Palace and Gardens, and then enjoyed a delightful, late afternoon Chopin concert in another Warsaw palace, performed especially for us, while we sipped champagne.

After Warsaw, we left Poland, crossing the German frontier at the River Oder on the way to Berlin. There was so much to see in Berlin, so much history that we Americans only heard about and saw in the newsreels about World War II during our childhood. The Brandenburg Gate, the Reichstag building (symbol of Hitler's rise to power), the remains of the Berlin Wall and the Checkpoint Charlie Museum, documenting nearly thirty years of dramatic escape attempts across the Iron Curtain, were just some of the historic sites we visited. Berlin at night came alive at a local restaurant with great musical entertainment and traditional Berliner cuisine.

Remains of the Berlin Wall

Phyllis and I had decided, before we came on this trip, that we had seen and enjoyed much of the Mediterranean delights; it was time to open our eyes and hearts and explore a very different area of Europe.

Prague was our next city on this historic journey, after heading for the Czech border high in the Ore Mountains. Our two days in Prague were filled with sightseeing trips. The Czech capital, Prague, is a city with a long and colorful cultural tradition. We needed more than two days to really absorb and enjoy all that Prague offered.

A view of one of the bridges over the Vltava River in Prague

After arriving in Prague, I received a phone call from my son, Cliff. He was also in Prague at the same time with his family. What a surprise! We didn't get to see him, as our schedule was so intense, and we had only one day left before leaving for Vienna.

Phyllis and I are history buffs and enjoyed seeing and learning so much about Eastern Europe. Our trip was anything but glamorous; it involved a lot of walking, climbing stairs, listening to guides, and sitting on buses for hours, but we loved it!

When we were in Vienna, we decided to include some shopping, as there had been very little time to do so; we shopped with a *vengeance.*

Returning to the USA, Phyllis and I knew travelling together would become an important part of our lives. In our winters in Florida, we rarely go without seeing each other every week; sometimes we get together two or three times in a week. We speak on the telephone almost every day. In the summer, Phyllis lives in Boston at her daughter's home; I live in my New York apartment. We are back and forth from New York to Boston throughout the summer months.

Having a relationship like ours is one of the most comforting aspects of our lives at this point in time. We can share everything and anything. I don't suggest the travelling created this closeness, but I think it brought to the surface something we always knew was there. It is a blessing; we are family.

In the fall of 2007, we planned our greatest undertaking . . . an adventure we would never forget. But that's another story.

How often have we heard, "Count your blessings?" Sometimes, it takes a rainy day to appreciate them.

I dedicate this tale to the loving, kind and selfless mothers of the world. *You know who you are.*

TODAY I NEEDED A GOOD CRY

HAVE YOU KEPT THE HAND-MADE cards, letters and comical but precious scribbles of your child's childhood? I hope so. They are reassuring consolation for the "good-cry-day." Take them out from time to time, and know you did a few things right.

Recently, I had just such a day. It was dreary, drizzly, cooler than usual, and a good day to tackle the job of cleaning out one of my storage closets.

When I reached for the large flower-printed box, the weight of it caused it to fall to the floor. Out spewed cards, letters and mementos from my children, from kindergarten through adulthood. I sat on the floor, for almost two hours, reading every word written long ago . . . and some in more recent years. The tears, running down my cheeks, kept pace with the rain.

My oldest child, Cliff, the serious one . . . probably written in first grade.
You are a good MoM and DaD. And
I Love you very much. Roseis
Are red Vilits are Blue if you
Were not my pairnts I would
Turne Blue.

Cliff . . . third year of college . . . twenty-one years old.

Dear Mom and Dad,
I cannot stop thanking you for all that you have done for me. No child has any right to request more or perhaps even as much as I have received from you. Best of all I know that you are doing all of this because of your love for me and your trust in me. I hope that I shall never again betray that trust, and plan to include your desires and wishes alongside, instead of subordinate to my own in most future decisions. Cliff

Happy Birthday Mom, after the death of his father. (Cliff)
> Happy Birthday Mom
> Dream beautiful thoughts, and believe.
> This is the gift you have given me.
> Thanks,
> I Love you

Today, Cliff is an attorney in Denver, Colorado, and the father of two children.

My middle child, Todd, the adorable "imp." With his sweet face and big blue eyes, he could "charm the pants off you" and you wouldn't even know it. Todd, from camp, 1969 . . . nine years old.

<u>FIRST CARD</u>
Send me lots of pretzels, popcorn, gum and candy. VERY FAST.
I give them out and I'm very popular.

<u>SECOND CARD</u>
Where is my package? If it doesn't come soon I'm going to kill you.

<u>THIRD CARD</u>
Finally! It came today. Love you very much.

Where's the goods? You're ruining my reputation

Todd, June, 1978 . . . eighteen years old.
Mom and Dad . . . Happy Anniversary

I've held on to this card for over a week now trying to find the right words to express the gratitude and love that I feel. This was no easy task. I guess the simplest way is to say thanks and tell you that I love and appreciate both of you very much. I realize that it didn't take a week to put it into words, but they're sufficient to convey the message.

I Love you

Todd . . . Mother's Day . . . early 1990s

Mother's Day is meant to celebrate mothers that are just like you: giving, caring and loving. Thanks for being a loving, supportive mother. It means the world to me.

Todd . . . Happy Birthday, Mom . . . 1990s

If words could express how I feel, I'd use them. Unfortunately, none could. Suffice it to say that I love every square inch of you.

Todd . . . Mother's Day, after the death of his father, early 2002

I bet you never thought you'd be a single parent. This is a very special Mother's Day for both of us. I love you very much! You are and always were a great mother.

My sons knew how much I loved flowers, and continued the tradition their father started by sending me flowers on most occasions.

One evening, upon returning home, I was greeted with a bouquet of breathtaking orchids and roses. Who could have sent me flowers? It wasn't my birthday or Mother's Day. The card read: Without you, I wouldn't be here. Love, Todd

It was March 10, the day of Todd's forty-eighth birthday.

Today, Todd is a financial advisor in New York City, and the father of two children.

My youngest child, Tina, was born when her brothers were six and nine years of age.

Tina was a "mommy's girl" from day one. She is my best friend and advisor, and can stop me in my tracks, whenever she feels I'm wrong or heading in a bad emotional direction. But, when she feels she's chastised me too severely, she quickly calls back to apologize. Even when it's not necessary.

After college, Tina came home to live with her parents, and then moved out a few years later.

Tina . . . first grade.
> To Mom and Dad
> I Love you so much
> I can't tell how much
> I do

Mother's Day . . . May 12, 1991 . . . twenty-five years old.

> This year has been a monumental one for me, what with moving out, and living on my own. I have made many decisions on my own accord, and I truly feel like I am a mature, responsible adult. This growth could not have happened without your love, support and counsel.
>
> Mom, I just want you to know how very much I love you, though I certainly don't tell you enough. As grown up and mature as I may claim to be, I will never stop being your daughter, and I will never forget what a loving, wonderful and talented mother I have. Someday, hopefully, she will be famous . . . as well!

Mother's Day . . . early 2000s . . . after the death of her father.

> Every day I thank God for the warmth, love and understanding I have grown up with. Mom, I thank <u>you</u> for teaching me how to love and to be myself. There are no words to say how very proud and lucky I am to have you for my mother. I guess it's simple, if not silly, but all I can say is . . .
> THANK YOU and I LOVE YOU
> I hope I'm just like you when I "grow up!"

Today, Tina is a chiropractor in Miami, Florida
I discovered the following in the over-crowded closet when I reached up to place the flower-printed box onto another shelf. It was stuffed under a pile of photographs. It was titled, "My Personal Biblette," by Tina Pearl.

The cover, made of red construction paper, was torn around the edges, as were most of the other pages. It was filled with photographs, certificates, cards and four chapters of her life.

I had never read them before. I was so touched by her writing and would like to share it with the readers of this book . . . with her permission.

I always knew her talent for writing songs, but never realized her talent for telling a story.

TINA'S STORY

CHAPTER I—MY GENESIS

In the beginning, I was very small and very impatient. On Monday morning of April 18, 1966, at 9:00 a.m., Tina Dawn arrived, four weeks early. Being the last child of Mona Sue and David Marcus Pearl, and being the only girl, I was treated like a princess. My brothers, Clifford Ross and Todd Evan, welcomed me with open arms. Although Todd, at six years old, was determined to throw any female child out the window, he had a change of heart the morning my mother left for the hospital.

CHAPTER II—MY INNOCENT YEARS

When my brothers were young, they used to go to sleep-away camp during the summer. Well, one summer, when Todd was ten, my parents and I saw him on visiting day. I was four years old at the time. Of course, when parents come, the camps like to show films of the children. In this particular film was a scene of my brother swimming. Now, Todd and I used to pretend we were married, so, when I saw him in the film, I screamed, "That's my husband!"

I used to have a little "boyfriend" when I was about eight years old. We used to lie in bed together, innocently. One day, my mom walked in and asked, "What are you doing?"

"Playing husband and wife," I replied.

CHAPTER III—SIBLING RIVALRY

Since my brothers are six and nine years older, I never had any memorable fights with them. Instead, I will tell you of another incident.

This past summer, I went away to Wellesley College to take some courses. Well, I had such a great time there, that I made dozens of friends. There was only one problem—I forgot my friends back home, including my boyfriend, Larry. I wrote to no one this summer, not Larry, or my friends, or my parents. When I got home, I called Larry. By this time, he had been going out with someone else for a month. It was then that I realized the full extent of the damage. By not bothering to write, I broke off a wonderful friendship between two people. We broke up and didn't speak to each other for a while after that.

CHAPTER IV-- RECONCILIATION

A month and a half later, we finally made up. About a month after I got home, I wrote Larry a letter of apology to let him know how much our friendship meant to me. I had been praying that he would accept me as a friend again, and those prayers were answered. Two and a half weeks after receiving the letter, he gave me a call. He had finally accepted my sincerest apology.

Good Friends

This is not the end, but only the beginning!

If you listen with your heart, not just your ears, you will learn some of the greatest truths from children.

Tina was fourteen years old when she wrote her "Biblette." I was touched by her sensitivity. When I put it back into the over-stuffed closet, one thought ran through my mind—*like mother, like daughter.*

When the last letter was read and my "good cry" was over, the sun came out and shone, not only outdoors, but in my heart as well.

I packed all the memories back into the flower-printed box, stored them in the over-crowded closet, and saved them for another "good-cry-day."

I washed my face, put on some makeup and stepped outside to face the world, knowing how blessed I truly was.

Negativity closes the door. A positive outlook opens the door, allowing the good to flow into one's life.

THE FEEL-GOOD DAY

I WOKE UP THIS MORNING with a *really* good feeling. Instead of pulling the covers up to my neck for another delicious, few minutes of sleep, I rolled out of bed invigorated, and headed to the kitchen for my first cup of coffee.

I sat in my father's chair (my father sat before the fireplace each evening when he came home from work, in his favorite chair) enjoying the first sips of my coffee, while reading my *Daily Word*, saying my prayers and meditating. The good feeling remained with me.

The phone rang. Checking the number before answering, I noticed it was unfamiliar. I decided not to answer it because I hated all those cold calls. But, on the last ring I picked it up, prepared to quickly hang up, when I heard a familiar voice. It was an old friend I had not spoken to for almost a year. We talked for over a half an hour, catching up on the details of our lives this past year. She was going to be in town next month and wanted to see me. Great! We made plans to get together.

After breakfast, showering and dressing, I grabbed my to-do list and left the house. My list was long and time was of the essence.

Driving around town, I made every green light—very unusual.

Stopping at the bank, I was first in line—again, very unusual.

Circling the parking lot at the mall is never a great experience. Within minutes, a woman pulled out, just three spots before the entrance to the mall . . . and I was right there.

I headed directly to the Clinique counter to replenish my favorite lipstick. "I'm sorry," said the salesperson, "we're out of that color."

"Please check again." I implored.

"Wait," she answered, "I found one. It was in the wrong place."

The entire day went my way. From the endearing phone call from an old friend in the morning, to speaking to my children, who all *sounded* good, to the evening I shared with my best friend at dinner.

When I retired that night, I thought about my day. Everything went <u>so</u> well. Two days earlier, I had my "good-cry-day." A "good cry" bathes the soul. *What a difference a day, or two, makes.*

I had watched my DVD of *The Secret* the day before; the book and the video are best sellers. I had watched it multiple times, but sometimes we need to be reminded about the positive position we assume in life. Could *The Secret* have been my "guardian angel" reminding me of the truth I already knew? It tells us that the secret is "the law of attraction."

Did I wake this morning feeling good because my positive attitude kicked in and attracted the good into my life?

I believe my subconscious mind absorbed the wonderful lessons of *The Secret*. One cannot just listen. One must learn to use the great lessons of life offered to us, whether in a book, a DVD, a CD or a lecture by those wiser than we are. The teachings of the Dalai Lama, Deepak Chopra and so many others offer us the opportunity to bring joy and peace into our lives. They teach us to listen to our inner wisdom. Listen, learn, absorb, and then utilize your wisdom.

I wish you many "feel-good" days.

Two little words, "thank you," can warm your mind, heart and soul as quickly as the blink of an eye.

HOW DO YOU SPELL "THANK YOU?"

IS "THANK YOU" SPELLED *Mom* or *Dad?* Thank you for giving me a memorable childhood and for being my guiding light, Mom, when I was lost in the dark. I still feel the freedom you gave me to be me.

I smile when I remember running, in my bare feet, through the potato fields of the farm up the road with my brothers. We were gathering potatoes, until the farmer began shooting his rifle in the air. Racing home, we dropped all the potatoes we had gathered.

You chastised us, but I never felt real anger. We promised never to do <u>that</u> again.

Your punishments were always fair, even though I may not have appreciated the fact at the time. But, your love was unconditional.

I tried to follow in your footsteps with my own family when I became a mother. Gratefully, much of it worked.

Is "thank you" spelled *David*, for being my husband and the love of my life, for always believing in me and telling me, almost every day, how much you loved me?

Thank you for working so hard, throughout your life, to provide for your family. You learned great work ethics at a young age. You were only eight years old when your mother went to work to help "put bread on the table." When you were in your early teens, you waited outside the supermarket to carry bundles and earn tips.

Living in a two bedroom Bronx apartment, you shared a room with your sister till she married.

You were determined to be successful, and you never gave up . . . and successful you became.

Thank you, my darling David, for giving our family a wonderful life. There were many sacrifices along the way, especially when you worked seven days a week to build your business.

You left this world too early, at the age of sixty-nine, but you left me secure. I can help our children in so many ways: in a business, in college educations for our grandchildren, in just some of the pleasures that make life more enjoyable. I can contribute to charities I deeply care for, and live a comfortable life, knowing that you are and always have watched over me. Thank you . . . thank you . . . thank you.

Could "thank you" be spelled in the names of my children, *Clifford* or *Todd* or *Tina*? They have rewarded me with so much love, appreciation, fulfillment and happiness.

Surely, I could spell "thank you" for the loyal and loving friends who were there for me when my husband David passed away. And for the love and caring they still bestow upon me to this day. These two little words, "thank you," can open the doors of your heart, urging you to give more of yourself.

My list could fill pages of the wonderful people—friends, relatives, acquaintances—even those who provide their service, personally or publically.

How often have we held open a door, picked up someone's dropped article, or let someone in line ahead of us, and never heard a "thank you?" This non-response elicits the exact opposite feeling . . . we are irked. Do these people have a sense of entitlement? I prefer to think they are so preoccupied, they aren't aware of our courteous gestures. Sometimes, I want to shout, *"Hello"* or *"Thank You,"* to wake someone up from their mental stupor.

"Thank you" are two little words that can never be over-used. They are fresh and new each time they are spoken.

Nothing is written in stone. Life, as well as the things that are so familiar to us, are as changeable as the tides. Change is inevitable. Go with the flow.

Stop The World—I Want To Get Off was a brilliant musical written in 1961 by Leslie Bricusse and Anthony Newley. We often spend our lives searching for more and better. In the end, we sometimes come to realize that what we had all along was all we ever needed. This was a lesson learned from this wonderful show.

STOP THE WORLD—I NEED TO GET OFF

WHAT EVER HAPPENED TO WRITING LETTERS? I'm not talking about texting or e-mails but just old-fashioned letters that one could keep, tucked away, and re-read whenever a whim prompted an old memory.

Press 1, press 2, press 3. My fingers get more exercise than the rest of me. Where are the humans that answered a phone and politely asked if they could help you? Are we becoming a world of robots? By the time a human answers, I forget what I want to say.

Cell phones. They started as a convenient form of communication. Today, they are so multi-faceted that one is able to push a button and turn on or off their lights, twenty miles from home. Soon they'll be able to start dinner before you get home. It seems like an entire encyclopedia is downloaded into the newest phones. Why bother to go to a library, or even a university—you could get a Master's degree from your cell phone!

Phone booths are extinct. People walk on the street attached to their earpiece, their mouths moving, and sometimes, they don't even know where they're going. They are so absorbed in conversation.

If you don't have the latest cell phone, you're a dinosaur.

Books! How I love to curl up in my favorite chair, clutching the latest hot novel, with a cup of tea and chocolate-chip cookies. Today, books are on CDs. You can hear the story while driving and pass your turnoff on the highway, finding yourself five miles out of your way. You may discover new territory you never visited before.

And the Kindle! Bookstores will eventually become obsolete. I still prefer holding a book, instead of a piece of plastic and metal with a screen. I love the feel of turning the pages.

TVs. They get bigger, but flatter. Who put them on a diet? You <u>must</u> have TiVo. God forbid you miss a program when you're out for the day or evening.

We now live in a virtual world—virtual cards; virtual communication; virtual dates; virtual postcards; virtual conversations; virtual letters; etc.

What happened to those wonderful days of sharing family time, when after dinner we played monopoly, bingo, cards, or just sat around talking to each other and telling stories? Today, time is absorbed with a volume of tasks: e-mails; Facebook; Twitter; YouTube; and much more.

Cars. They're sleeker and faster, more powerful than ever. I wonder if a horse and carriage, zooming at ninety miles an hour, ever cut off another horse and carriage driving somewhat slower. What were the curse words in those days?!?

We've been to the moon, and we continue to explore the universe. Progress is important, but all is speeding up like a runaway train.

Computers. Love them and hate them! How often have you heard, "The computers are down, please call back later," from a company you called to resolve a problem? Don't they have written records anymore? And what happens when your own computer crashes? FUN!!

Oh well! If you can't fight them, join them. I confess to partaking of many of the advantages of new technology. A new cell phone, computer, TV; sometimes even a car without a GPS is out of date almost before you buy it. It's getting quite expensive.

Okay, world, I promise not to jump off, but could you just slow down a little?

Gather people in the "springtime" of your life; nourish their acquaintance in the "summer." Reap their true friendship in the "autumn," and feel the warmth of their love in the "winter" of your waning years.

CALL ME "FRIEND"

WEBSTER'S DICTIONARY DEFINES "friend" as a person attached to another by feelings of affection or personal regard; a supporter; a person who is on good terms with another.

The words "love" and "loyalty" are left out of the equation. In my personal dictionary, these two words are most important.

Relationships are divided into multiple categories. There are acquaintances, casual friends, close friends, life-long friends and bosom buddies.

Growing up in a small town, my best friend married at the age of nineteen, and moved away. We had been inseparable—sleeping over each other's homes, sharing all the holidays, doing homework together and spending hours on the telephone, even though we lived only a few blocks apart.

I finally saw my friend again thirty years later, when she came home to visit her family.

The memory of the evening of the junior prom has always stayed with me. My best friend had a date for the prom and I did not. But I spent the day decorating the gym, in preparation of the evening to come. My best friend cancelled her date, because of me, and we went to the movies. That is a true example of friendship.

Sadly, after seeing her again, after thirty years, we had grown so far apart. There was little left of the old relationship. We had little in common. She had married a career soldier and lived on army bases in the Midwest. We corresponded for a while, and then lost touch. We parted politely, and never saw each other again.

I often regret having let go of some of my childhood friends and college friends. Somehow, after I married and had children, my life got caught in a swirling eddy, constantly moving. I reconstructed and built many homes in different locations. I now live in my thirteenth home since I left my parents' house, more than fifty-five years ago.

The winter of my life came too quickly, but I fortunately reaped many enduring friendships in the autumn.

When a woman becomes widowed or divorced, she is out of the comfort zone of the couples' world. She can still maintain her relationships with some of her closest couple friends, but her position is on a different level.

I've learned a great truth since I was widowed . . . *women take care of women.*

When a *dear* friend calls at 6:30 in the morning, tells you she is very ill, and asks if you can take her to the hospital, you jump out of bed, throw on your clothes, don't wash your face and, perhaps, don't even brush your teeth. You're there in twenty minutes.

When a *dear* friend calls to *talk*, because she's depressed and needs to vent, even though you need to shower, dress, put on makeup, and be out of the house within the hour . . . you listen. You call your appointment and tell them you're running late. Then you continue the conversation on your cell phone, from the car, or promise to call as soon as you return home. If the situation is very serious, if need be, you cancel your day or evening to be with her.

When a *dear* friend, who is alone, calls to ask what you're doing on Saturday night or Friday or any night, and you have plans, you ask her the same question. When the response is "nothing," you ask her to join you with your friend or friends, telling her she is very welcome. If you have tickets for an event, you try to get another ticket. If you can't then you make other arrangements to see each other as soon as possible, letting her know you miss her.

When a *dear* friend is renovating her home, and needs to move out for several months, then informs you she will, temporarily, be living in a hotel, you give her the keys to your home and welcome her with, "Mi casa es su casa."

When a *dear* friend loses her mate though death or divorce, the need to be with that friend, as much as possible, is crucial during this period. Cry together—it cleanses the soul. As time passes, if your friend remains alone, but you have new companionship in your life, you never give up the time you share with your friend because of your new relationship.

When a *dear* friend needs you to accompany her to an important doctor, lawyer or other appointment, and your day is scheduled with a social agenda, you say yes, without letting her know there is any inconvenience.

Some of the above examples of *true friendship* may sound somewhat extreme. Believe me . . . I've been there. Have I always been a "true" friend?

Probably not. I know at times I have been, and I strive to continue to give the love and loyalty I feel for those I call *dear friends*.

Every woman needs only one *dear friend* to whom she can complain, bitch, cry, moan and laugh.

But, making new friends is refreshing. Keep yourself open.

Sometimes, we meet people along our way and we just "click." We feel as if we have known that new person for a lifetime, and often wish we had. Perhaps the timing was right for a new relationship.

Never stop seeking new friends. It can enrich your life.

The value of friendship is something we often take for granted and don't always appreciate as much when we are young. As time passes, we come to realize friendships are a treasure. We need to nourish our friendships and keep them healthy.

I believe the expression "bosom buddies" was coined for those who rest upon your heart.

The real voyage of discovery consists not in seeking new landscapes but in having new eyes.

—Marcel Proust

ADVENTURE BECKONS: HEED THE CALL

SOUTH AFRICA HAD BEEN on the dream list of places that Phyllis and I most wanted to visit. We decided in October, 2007, that we would fulfill that dream. In my David's words, "If not now, when?"

The search for the best safaris, places to visit, and who to use to plan our trip was quite extensive. My dear friend Merle, who had previously arranged wonderful trips for me, was given the task.

After weeks of researching, Merle found a company called African Classic Encounters located in New York City. The woman who owned the agency was South African. She advised us to spend our planned three weeks in South Africa alone, and not travel to Kenya or Tanzania, explaining that South Africa was a sizeable country and had so much to see and enjoy. She suggested we leave the visiting of other African countries for another time. And she was so right! Phyllis and I were not prepared for the adventures that lay ahead.

We left on October 7th from Atlanta to Johannesburg, on a private, specially designed trip for just the two of us.

It was dark and rainy upon arriving in Johannesburg the following afternoon. We were met at the airport and were driven to Pretoria to spend the night at Illyria House, a magnificent colonial manor. On our drive to Pretoria the sun came out and a brilliant rainbow arched itself across the landscape. Rainbows are my good-luck omen. I turned to Phyllis and said, "We are in for an incredible journey."

Illyria House is the secret retreat of royalty, heads of state and celebrities. Phyllis and I felt like two queens, having all our needs attended to. The suite we stayed in was finer than most five-star hotels with a balcony overlooking a garden. There were perhaps two other couples staying at the manor. Phyllis remarked, "I could get used to this kind of luxury." I concluded that I could, too!

Illyria House in Pretoria

After breakfast the following morning we were transferred to Capitol Station for departure on the elegant Rovos Rail. Phyllis and I shared a deluxe suite on the Pride of Africa, a seventy-two-passenger, elegant train that captured the romance and atmosphere of a bygone era, while experiencing the magic and mystery of Africa. We fantasized we would encounter Detective Hercule Poirot while we were part of the filming of *Murder on the Orient Express*. Fortunately, there were no murders.

Phyllis and me on the Rovos Rail . . . a toast to the adventure ahead of us

We enjoyed two exciting, luxurious days aboard the Pride of Africa, on our journey to Cape Town. Dining aboard was five-star, and we slept like babies being rocked to sleep with the rhythmic movement of the train. We had two stops along the way.

The first excursion brought us to Kimberly, home of the famous Big Hole and mine museum, which began with the diamond rush in 1871. The Big Hole is the largest manmade hole in the world. The digging yielded 14.5 million carats of diamonds. It was here that the famous Star of Africa was found, a magnificent 83.5-carat diamond, and it is the home of the well-known De Beers Consolidated Diamond Mines and the capital of the world's diamond industry.

Phyllis and I thought diamond tiaras would be nice for the two queens that we were, but we thought we would appear a little too ostentatious.

We bought nothing, but enjoyed a very interesting day.

On our second day, we disembarked the train and walked five kilometers into Matjiesfontein, the former headquarters of the British forces, where the train met us. We had a choice of remaining on the train or walking the distance; we needed the exercise.

The memory of our train trip remains with Phyllis and me to this day. We often reminisce about the incredible scenery, the elegant dining, the relaxation and fine service and the wonderful accommodations. We especially remember our dining experience. The train had two dining rooms, one casual and one more elegant. We decided we would try each one on the two nights aboard. On the second night, we dined in the elegant restaurant. Phyllis chose the table, but within fifteen minutes two couples entered the dining car and asked if we wouldn't mind changing our table, as they had dined at our table the night before and would like to dine there again. Phyllis, in her own inimitable way, politely told them "NO." They were very rude, pushy and quite unhappy, but Phyllis stuck to her guns, even after they asked us multiple times. *Hurrah*, Phyllis! I still laugh when I recall Phyllis dealing with those unpleasant people that evening.

We finally arrived in Cape Town, early evening on the second day, and were escorted to the Cape Grace Hotel.

We were completely awed by Cape Town. There is so much to tell about this fabulous city that I am speechless . . . *and that doesn't happen often.* Fortunately we had five wonderful days to explore Cape Town and its surroundings.

The Cape Grace Hotel sat on the waterfront with a magnificent view of Table Mountain. A short walk along the waterfront ended at a thriving, exciting mall, with excellent restaurants, taverns, cinemas, theaters and beautiful, contemporary shops overlooking the water. We dined on springbok and eland steaks, *bobotie* (a version of Shepherd's pie), kingklip and snoek (fishes), and ostrich, and ended with Rooibos tea . . . all quite good. When in Rome or Africa, do as the natives do. The beat of African music reverberating across the water from the mall, until late into the evening, reached our room, lulling us to sleep.

We awoke the following morning with exhilaration, anxious to start our exciting day. Our guide met us in the lobby after breakfast and told us the plan for the day. We were starting out on the cable car to the top of Table Mountain, a flat-topped mountain. Weather conditions were important, as the cable cars did not run when it was dangerously windy or the mountain was wrapped in the cloud known as the "tablecloth." Table Mountain is a place of dramatic scenic beauty, and one of South Africa's most famous landmarks, overlooking Cape Town. It is visible from as far as 125 miles out to sea. The cable car ride is no more than five minutes, but the views of the city, the Cape peninsula, the coastline and the ocean are spectacular, and can be seen from eleven viewpoints on the summit. We hiked the 1.8-mile width on the top, enjoying the 1,470 species of diverse flora and a range of fauna. It was thrilling! We both concurred that we were so delighted at our choice of coming to South Africa. Although we both loved Europe and the areas of the Mediterranean, experiencing a new culture and a totally different landscape was very exciting.

Table Mountain with the Cape Grace Hotel along the waterfront

Returning to the hotel, our guide informed us that we were going on a Cape Town City tour and then on to Kirstenbosch National Botanical Garden, set against the eastern slopes of Table Mountain. The gardens grew only indigenous South African plants, some of which we had never seen, but were magnificent.

Our day ended with a wonderful dining experience in our hotel, one of the finest dining options in town. We couldn't wait to retire for the evening and wake up to another exciting experience the following day. Each day was a gift, and each one more exciting than the previous day.

We slept late that following morning, as we had a day of leisure, and decided to explore the many markets after breakfast. We strolled along the waterfront, stopping at the many stands, and purchased strands of malachite from a native who was busy stringing the lovely green stones as we watched. We loved the music of the local bands along the waterfront and enjoyed the rhythmic beat. The music was *infectious*. We walked along . . . NO . . . we danced along our merry way.

The African Dream Marimba Band along the waterfront

They've got the rhythm; they've got the beat

After an early lunch, we were lucky to get tickets for the boat ride to Robben Island. Robben Island was originally an asylum and leper colony and was used since 1960 as a prison primarily for political prisoners, political troublemakers, social outcasts and the unwanted of society. President Nelson Mandela was in prison here for many of his twenty-seven years of incarceration. We entered the cell in which he lived for many of those years, and could almost feel his presence. How does one survive so many years incarcerated, and then become the president of a nation and receive the Nobel Peace Prize? He was a lesson for all of us. Hold on to your beliefs and never give up.

Walking through the camp, and viewing the photographs and reading the documents, we felt as if we were visiting another concentration camp. Some of the documents touched us deeply.

Examples: A Woman's Place is in the Struggle . . . NOT BEHIND BARS.

FREE THE CHILDREN: The declaration of children's rights

The prisoners of Robben Island succeeded on a psychological and political level in turning the prison into a symbol of freedom. Robben Island came to symbolize the triumph of the human spirit over enormous adversity, not only for the entire African continent, but for the entire world.

The following morning began early when we left for a full-day private tour of Cape Peninsula. It was truly a tour of breathtaking beauty and a glimpse of some of the most expensive real estate in South Africa. Our route took us along the Atlantic Ocean, along Marine Drive, stretching down to Hout Bay which is a quaint fishing village on the Atlantic seaboard, and over Chapman's Peak Drive, on to Cape Point, where the Indian and the Atlantic Oceans meet. We then arrived at the Cape of Good Hope. We felt as if we had almost reached the end of the world and it was beautiful.

Phyllis and me at the Cape of Good Hope

After leaving the Cape of Good Hope we continued on south over Chapman's Peak Drive, following the Atlantic Ocean on to Fish Hoek. Then we encountered the Indian Ocean again and drove north along the ocean to see the Jackass Penguin Colony at Boulders Beach near Simon's Town. The sight of hundreds of penguins was spectacular. I think one of the young penguins took a liking to me, as he left his group, called a waddle, and ventured over to "talk" to me. *We had a delightful conversation.* Phyllis laughed when she watched me talking to a penguin.

A waddle of penguins at Boulders Beach

A chat with my newfound "friend"

On the way to Cape Peninsula and the Cape of Good Hope, we encountered a troop of baboons across the road. They were cute, but very wild, and we were warned not to feed them, as they are dangerous and are attracted by food. Two of the little devils climbed on the hood of the van as we stopped to observe them.

Wild baboons on the way to Cape Peninsula

After breakfast the next day we were taken on a full day tour of the Winelands. The countryside was beautifully scenic. Then we continued travelling north to the cultural center of the Winelands, and then on to the Paarl Valley.

We stopped at many wineries for wine tastings, including KWV, at one time the largest wine co-operative in South Africa, and then arrived at Tokara, where we enjoyed a wonderful lunch and stunning views of the valley. By the time we left Phyllis and I were bleary-eyed. We were not used to imbibing during the day, and *snoozed* most of the way back to Cape Town.

We fell asleep early that night, our last night in Cape Town. We didn't want to leave, but a new adventure awaited us the following morning. We both vowed to return to Cape Town some day; there was so much more to do and see. We agreed that Cape Town was on top of the list of places that deserved a return visit.

We left Cape Town the following morning on our way to Bushmans Kloof, the site of our first safari. The trip took us to the West Coast National Park at Langebaan, where we stopped to view rare bird life; there are over 250 bird species in the park. We continued northwards via the Olifants River

Valley through the Cederberg Mountains, driving over the Pakhuis Pass to reach our final destination: Bushmans Kloof Private Nature Preserve. The drive was awesome! Phyllis and I had never been on a safari before; we didn't know what to expect. We were delightfully surprised. Our accommodations were roomy and lovely. The dining was sheltered outside and was more luxurious than we had anticipated. The food was pretty good, too!

In the early evening, we were taken on a sundowner drive to view the wildlife, while we enjoyed cocktails and hors d'oeuvres on the back of our open safari vehicle. The following day I made sure to have my camera out and ready. I took over seven hundred photographs while travelling throughout South Africa.

A herd of springbok grazing in the early morning

Two Zebras, sharing their morning repast

Two Bonteboks end-to-end . . . a pair of "bookends"

The following day was exciting in a different way. We hiked the reserve while our guide led us to the Fallen Rock Cave. The walls were covered with scenes that appeared prehistoric. Archaeologists guess that the paintings are anywhere between three and ten thousand years old. The difficulty in pinpointing the age is because of the red paint. They can carbonate the surface of the rock but not the stain left behind when the paint wears away.

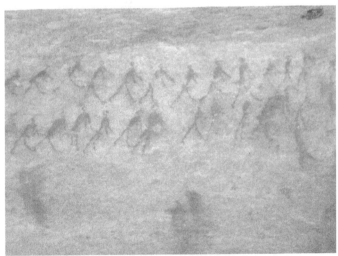

Prehistoric rock art scene of perhaps dancers

The afternoon was a photographer's dream. The rock formations were nothing like we had ever seen in the United States. I couldn't stop photographing everything in sight, including little animals hiding among the formations. Phyllis left the photography up to me, as I had recently bought a digital camera and was fascinated by the many ways it took pictures. My husband, David, was the photographer in the family and now it was my turn. I promised Phyllis she would have copies of the entire trip. I confess, I still have not downloaded them onto her computer, but I will be doing it shortly. Writing about it now has jolted my memory and triggered my guilt into not having done it sooner.

Beautiful purples running through a boulder

A little African dormouse hiding among the boulders

South Africa is truly a magnificent country, and again, we hated to leave Bushmans Kloof, but Birkenhead was awaiting us. After breakfast, we took the road to Hermanus on our way to Birkenhead House, a beautiful retreat for the soul, perched high on the cliffs of Hermanus overlooking the sea. It was the peak season for whale watching and we could observe the frolicking whales right from our hotel. The day after we arrived, we were taken to Walker Bay in Hermanus, a whale watcher's paradise. It is here that people come from all over to enjoy watching several species of whales up close.

A pod of five whales in Walker Bay

On Sunday, the following day, we remained at Birkenhead, as Phyllis had caught a virus and was laid up for a day. The good sport that she was, she didn't let on how miserable she was the day before. Remaining at Birkenhead was not difficult to take, as it was a magnificent place for R&R. Although she wanted me to dine in their beautiful restaurant overlooking the sea, I would not leave her, and we both dined in our room, till she was able to get out of bed and continue our adventure.

Photo taken from our room; it doesn't begin to show this magnificent place

Monday morning we were taken to Cape Town International for a flight to Johannesburg. We then connected to a flight to Hoedspruit on our way to the safari area. We were met at the airport and transferred by road to Camp Jabulani, an elephant-back safari camp in the Kapama Game Reserve. We were unaware of the elegance that awaited us upon arrival. There were six secluded, luxurious suites, each with its own splash pool and private deck, a lounge with a fireplace, and every amenity one would expect in a five-star hotel. The camp also offered a gym and a spa.

A view of the elegant interior of Camp Jabulani

After a gourmet dinner on the terrace, we retired to our beautiful suite for a restful night's sleep. It had been a long day, and tomorrow held a totally new experience . . . riding an elephant. Upon my pillow was this lovely note, which spoke so eloquently of Africa.

As the velvet stillness of
the African night
descends over our world,
may I wish you a
peaceful slumber to
awaken to the sounds
of the African bush as
it summons the morning
dawn

I don't know who composed this, but it spoke the truth . . . we were awakened by the sounds of Africa, but had enjoyed a peaceful night's rest.

In the morning we were taken to where thirteen trained elephants and their grooms resided. Jabulani, the lead elephant, was brought to the camp as an orphaned baby. The camp was, afterwards, named after him. I was given the privilege and honor of riding Jabulani. His groom brought Jabulani over to meet me. The elephant laid his trunk in my hand and as I petted him, I was told that an elephant never forgets; he would remember me if I returned ten years later.

Before our trip began, Phyllis said, "I'm not riding an elephant."

"Yes you are," was my reply.

The *no I'm nots* and the *yes you ares* went back and forth. I hoped that when we finally got to the elephant camp, she would change her mind. I was so proud of her when she climbed on her elephant and strode away with a big smile on her face.

Riding Jabulani with his handler

Male Nyala, a medium-sized antelope

The vantage point was incredible. Since elephants move silently and in a single file through the bush, one is able to view game in close proximity. My camera didn't stop. The Nyala was the first animal we observed. Safaris ended with sundowners in the bush.

A curious giraffe wandering in the bush

A pod of elephants arriving for a drink at their water hole

A warthog, one of the ugliest animals I encountered. A warthog can live in areas without water for several months of the year.

A family of elephants strolling in the bush—mama, papa and the kids

After lunch, we departed on a game drive in an open safari vehicle to view more of the "big five"—buffalo, elephant, leopard, lion and rhinoceros—and a variety of smaller wildlife. We viewed them all, but the most exciting and a surprise to all, including our game ranger, was finding the "King of the Jungle" relaxing on the roadside. Our ranger told us he had never seen one that size or coloring before. The lion was a deep taupe color instead of the usual camel tone, with a large black mane. We sat in our vehicle a few yards away observing him for about twenty-five minutes. I begged the lion to roar, so I could capture it on my digital video camera. Our ranger said the lion won't roar when he's being observed. I pleaded with the lion, and then, he roared continuously for about two minutes. I caught it all on video and everyone applauded. Phyllis was astounded and laughed heartily. I knew what was going through her head: *Mona never gives up.*

King of the Jungle

The following morning we took a forty-minute drive from Camp Jabulani through the bush to the Hoedspruit Endangered Species Center. It was also a Cheetah Research Center. The center was a fascinating place where we observed many different animals in captivity, including a tiger from India. There are no tigers in South Africa. The highlight of the day was petting

Phyllis and I, petting the "pet" cheetah

the cheetah. I snuggled up to it, as it was raised as a cub and as "domesticated" as a wild animal could be. It was really sweet! I didn't think Phyllis would be comfortable getting so close to the cheetah, but I was amazed and delighted to see her feeding and petting the beautiful animal. Sometimes she astounds me.

We also witnessed a scene of African wild dogs eating the carcasses of dead animals, while the vultures sat high above in the treetops, awaiting their opportunity to swoop down and finish the leftovers. The vultures play a role in cleaning up the dead and decaying carcasses, which helps to remove centers of disease.

The African wild dogs—first in line for breakfast

The vultures waiting their turn to enjoy breakfast

The next morning, before breakfast, we took an early safari on our elephants. I was happy to see Jabulani again. He came right over to me and nuzzled my hand. We proceeded into the bush for some early morning sightings. It was still a little hazy, but we sighted giraffes nibbling the treetops for their morning repast, some rhinos and a herd of buffalo. After breakfast I said goodbye to Jabulani, and begged him not to forget me. Phyllis couldn't stop talking about her wonderful experience riding an elephant. I promised to report her adventure and her agility to her family. She rode like a "trooper."

After leaving Camp Jabulani, we enjoyed a magnificent, panoramic sightseeing tour on our way to our last safari at the Singita Private Game Preserve. We travelled through breathtaking scenery, including God's Window, Blyde River Canyon, Bourke's Luck Potholes, Pilgrim's Rest (the first gold-mining town in South Africa), and the areas of Sabi, Hazyview and Mpumalanga.

God's Window and Blyde River Canyon

When we finally arrived at the Singita Boulders Lodge, we were again surprised and delighted at the luxurious accommodations and the beauty of the lodge. Singita lies within the Sabi Sand Game Preserve and borders Kruger National Park. It has traversing rights over 15,000 hectares of big game territory. There are no fences to separate Singita from Kruger National Park. The animals are free to roam as they please, which creates the perfect

Women on the road to Singita

setting for viewing the diversity of the wildlife.

There was so much to enjoy: bush dinners under the stars, game viewing and walks with knowledgeable guides, river hikes, dinner in the "boma" around a campfire, and so much more. The lodge rests in the heart of the private game reserve on the banks of the Sand River. In all our years of travelling and residing in beautiful hotel suites, Phyllis and I had never experienced a suite like the one at the Singita Boulders Lodge.

Left—huge twin beds placed together.
Right—fireplace between bedroom and living room.
The suite was the size of an apartment in New York City.
Dining was a gastronomic delight

The following morning we departed on our first game drive with a very experienced ranger and a tracker sitting on a high seat up front, above the safari vehicle.

Leopard resting on a hill, waking up to the early morning light

We tracked through the bush, greeting all the animals early in the morning . . . a very good time for viewing most of the wildlife before the heat of the day settled in.

A family of rhinos sharing breakfast

A herd of Cape Buffalo, curious to see who came to visit early in the morning

Female Nyala antelopes out for a morning stroll

Later that day we went on a hike with our ranger, and discovered some fascinating facts about the Augrabies lizards. The young male lizards imitate females to fool aggressive older males into leaving them alone. They delay displaying the vibrant colors of the sexually mature male until they are able to defend themselves. They are, perhaps, the original "transvestites."

Augrabies lizards sunning themselves

There was so much to photograph, I would have to turn this book into a photographic memoir, which in a way it was. Shortly after finding the lizards, we came upon a herd of impalas.

A herd of impalas amassing for a big powwow

We later discovered three hippos floating in the water. They refused to come out to be photographed, so we took pictures of their chubby faces. They stared at us, as if to say, "You're intruding upon our privacy while we're relaxing in our bathtub."

A family of hippos enjoying their swim

Our ranger informed us that hippos spend much of their life submerged. They could almost be classified as amphibians; they conduct all their business under water, including mating and territorial fights. The water also protects their sensitive skin from the sun. The skin of hippos is thinner than it looks, and when they are out of the water for too long on a hot day, their skin can dry out and begin to crack.

On our last day, I mentioned to Phyllis that I was surprised that I had not seen any monkeys. Twenty minutes later, a group of monkeys appeared on the deck outside our room, sipping the water from the small pool on the deck. I took their photo as we left our room on our way to our farewell lunch.

Monkeys sitting on the fence outside our room

270

We lunched on the large, open verandah, with huge trees shading us from the intense sun. The monkeys were sitting in the trees above us, and suddenly, one monkey leaped upon the table next to us and grabbed the bread out of the hand of a woman about to put it in her mouth. Nasty! Everyone gasped, and began to laugh.

Walking back to our room, one of the office workers met up with us. I mentioned that it was interesting that I finally got to see monkeys on the day we were leaving. She said, "If you want to see monkeys, come with me," and took us to a large swimming pool. Monkeys were everywhere. I reached for my camera, about to photograph a lone monkey as he stared at me with a mean look, then suddenly I was attacked by the whole group. I began to run as they grabbed onto my pants, trying to bite my ankles.

The "stand-off," staring down the monkey

The monkeys, just before the attack

271

I made it back to my room safely, but vowed never to stare down a monkey ever again. They may be cute, but they are not very friendly creatures, especially those wild in South Africa.

Afterwards, we were transferred to the Singita Airstrip for our flight to Johannesburg. We said our farewells to Africa as we boarded our international flight back to the USA. Our experiences in South Africa were so diverse and memorable that Phyllis and I still refer to our journey as the trip of a lifetime. Our only sad disappointment was that our husbands missed this great adventure.

Aging and gravity . . . two cohorts playing the same game. Who can win first?

I NEED TO HAVE A TALK WITH GRAVITY

GRAVITY, LISTEN UP. I've been very good all these years. I have respected your position and gone along with your demands.

I've exercised, kept my muscles strong and even though you tried to pull them down, they remained tight and uplifted.

My figure, face and hair have managed pretty well. Until you decided it was time to do your thing. Okay. A girl is entitled to a little "uplift" at least once in her lifetime. No disrespect to you.

Haven't felt well lately and lost some pounds. Why does weight loss start from the top down instead of from the bottom up?

My face looks too thin, and all the exercising that raised my bust . . . forget it! My "boobs" dropped, but my butt is still intact . . . full force.

I find more hair in the sink every day. Are you pulling it out one strand at a time? If you're collecting hair, between me and my friends, you could weave a pretty big rug.

Would it be too much to ask if you could take some time off to give us ladies a break?

I know I'm supposed to age gracefully, and I accept that. But, I could use a little help from your direction. I've got to stay in the "game."

I don't enjoy living at the cosmetic surgeon's and being poked with needles to fill every nook and cranny, but a girl needs some TLC.

Let's face it, gravity: I'm not in competition with you. I don't plan on staying around as long as you, but, have a heart. Do you ever take time off?

I've often heard the expression, "Your script is written the day you are born." I prefer to believe you write your own script. Scripts can be revised. We are our own directors and producers.

THE SCRIPT OF LIFE

WE RISE IN THE "EAST" of our souls, and *set* in the "West." In the interim, we live the spectrum of our emotions. Our minds continually write our script, day by day, sometimes getting out of control.

When I'm asked to give advice to my family or dear friend, I tend to think more clearly than when I give advice to myself. Perhaps this is because the problem is not entrenched in my already overloaded, filing cabinet brain.

We <u>must</u> take control. I've discovered that partaking in meditation and prayer each morning helps me to center myself. I can approach a problem with calmer, more assured attitude, that I <u>can</u> work things out for a better outcome.

Sometimes, we sit on the high side, sometimes we slip to the low. Balancing in the center of the see-saw we call life usually works best.

Does this outlook always work one hundred percent of the time? NO! If it works eighty or even seventy percent, I'm satisfied. I've learned to deal with the other twenty or thirty percent.

The advantage of advancing years is having lived so many different situations that you realize how many times you worried for the most inane things. They usually worked themselves out . . . all by themselves. Save your emotional and mental energy for the really important issues.

I belong to a "Search for Meaning" class. We meet once a week, and discuss all sorts of issues. We're a group of about twenty women. Our leaders, and sometimes the participants, suggest excellent books to read, which help us to help ourselves. We're a wonderful group, and often help each other just by sharing our experiences, both good and bad.

There are common threads running throughout our lives. No matter what level of circumstance we live, there is always a shred of something that we can relate to in the lives of others. It brings us together so we know we are never alone. We are all swimming in this vast ocean of life; some of us reach the shore before others. But, most of us eventually make it to shore if we don't give up.

I would suggest that anyone interested in bettering their emotional health gather a group of friends together and hold a similar class. It can be done in one's home, starting off with a small group, and when it catches on, it will grow.

I believe we <u>can</u> change our scripts. It's not easy . . . it takes work. But, if we are willing to learn new, more positive ways to deal with the script we've been handed, we can make great strides.

People like Tony Robbins are excellent examples of those who made the determination to make their life scripts better.

This is not an essay on self-improvement. This is how <u>I</u> have come to terms with my own script and have employed many of the lessons I have learned.

Some of them are:

Be good to myself. If not me . . . who should be? Be good to others, too!

When I try too hard to change others, I must stop, and realize the change that is needed is within myself.

Don't assume anything till you know the truth. You may be pleasantly surprised . . . or quite disappointed.

I strive to be right . . . not for others, but for myself.

Never look at what you don't have. Open your heart, your mind, and your eyes, and see what you do have.

You don't have to agree with everyone. You only have to agree to respect each other's point of view. Keep an open mind. And listen!

The list could fill an entire book. If you are reading this, you already know many of them. But, all of us could reach for more knowledge to enrich our lives.

I discovered that writing letters is a way of dealing with some difficult relationships. Perhaps, because I write regularly, the written word comes easily to me.

The beauty of writing a letter to resolve a conflict or terminate a relationship is that you are not interrupted; there is no confrontation; and you can never be accused of saying something you didn't say. There it is in black and white. It can be read over, and over, and over, without any words being changed.

The important point is to never put in writing what you may regret. Choose your words carefully. Get your point across, and be honest but never mean. Always end your letter with wishing the person well, even if you no longer wish to continue the relationship.

I believe everyone "fights the funk." Many of us can resolve our problems by ourselves. But, when life gets too difficult to handle, we need to cleanse the "bowels of our minds," and seek help from those trained to help us help ourselves. Talking it out is often the most cleansing therapy. A professional is a good start, but sometimes, even letting go and talking to a wise friend helps.

Work on your script. You may not earn an Oscar, but you can receive an Honorable Mention for a life well lived.

I am a miser of my memories of you and will not spend them.
  —Witter Bynner, "Coins"

I REMEMBER

I REMEMBER HOW WE LOVED to dance, and the look on your face as you held me close.

I remember how we loved the movies. You would become very emotional sometimes, and even cry. I love a man who cries.

I remember, David, how we enjoyed fly-fishing in the streams in Colorado.

I remember how we bravely skied down the slopes of mountains from Colorado to Switzerland, laughing and pretending to be fearless.

I remember travelling the world with you, when the romance was as exciting as the trip.

I remember our disagreements, and sometimes our battles, when I didn't want to talk to you for days. You always found a way to bring me back. The "making up" made up for it. I often hear women speak about their deceased husbands as "saints." You were no "saint," David. But, you were the great love of my life.

I remember how you loved bringing home little gifts to surprise me. When I asked you why, and said it wasn't my birthday or anniversary, Mother's Day or Valentine's Day, your response was, "I don't need an occasion to show you I love you."

I remember the excitement you felt when each of our children was born. You had so much love to give.

I remember you as Grandpa. You adored our grandchildren, and even though they lived in different states, you tried to see them as often as possible.

I remember how proud you were whenever I was complimented for any of my endeavors. You were always captain of my cheering squad . . . president of my fan club.

I remember how special you made me feel, just by being your wife.

I remember how much I loved you.

Create a true connection of love with your mind, body and soul, and never say, "I love you," unless you mean it.

THE CONNECTION

I'VE LEARNED MANY TRUTHS as the years rolled by. I've learned the importance of loyalty, charity, friendship, sharing, listening, compassion, faith—the list is endless. But one truth has loomed over me in these waning years. It is the truth of connection.

When your child is born and that tiny infant is laid in your arms, your body resonates with the beautiful warmth of pure love. Flesh against flesh...that is the truth of connection.

When you hug your children, whether they are small or grown-up, the hug, body against body, creates the warmth of love. That is the truth of connection.

When you greet your best friend, arms wrapped around each other, you feel totally connected. Your senses tell you, *I really love this person.*

I share these insights, not because I need to awaken the reality of these connections with my readers—you already know this—but because I wish to share my awareness of true love...the real connection. I realize that I have always innately known it and lived it, so why am I focused on these thoughts now? Perhaps age allows me the freedom to express my thoughts and my feelings about sex, love and the real connection.

Living in a community in Florida, where the average ages range from the 60s to the 80s, I love to see older couples holding hands. I delight in observing this "connection" at any age.

I love watching older couples dining alone and still talking to each other across the table, not just eating and glancing around the room to find something more of interest other than their table mate.

Why do I choose to focus on older couples? Is it because when a couple has lived together for a long period of time, the connection of history remains, but the connection of "real love" can often be fragmented? When I observe the unbroken connection of the two, my heart warms.

I've asked myself, why did God make sex pleasurable? Was it just to give us the incentive to keep the world going...to procreate? Or did God have more in mind?

The act of sexual intercourse becomes the most gratifying when the heart, the mind and the soul join the body. It is then that we have truly "connected." Without the first three ingredients, sex becomes no more than physical gratification. *Of course* this is important, but is this love?

The "real connection" remains even after the physical act of sex is no longer possible, if the heart, the mind and the soul were shared throughout the years of love-making. Sex can be the mainstay of a relationship, whether it is in or out of a marriage. But it doesn't always constitute love.

Sex is the most beautiful component of a true loving relationship when all the factors, heart, mind, body and soul work together. It remains the king (or queen) of the "love connection."

I've come to realize that I have lived my life with this quotient, but have recently realized the importance of this connection between two people who share this "formula." Perhaps, as one grows older, one reflects on the most important aspects of one's life.

The need to connect with another, physically, mentally and emotionally never ends. To hear that you are loved and admired for your mind, your body, your spirit, makes you feel whole. That is the "true connection."

It is this connection that makes life so gratifying. To have experienced it once is a gift. To have enjoyed this gift more than once is to have found life's treasure. I have a feeling this is what God had in mind.

Stay connected! Live your life with true love.

"It's not over till the fat lady sings."

No one knows where the adage originally came from, but it expresses the thought that you don't know how something ends until it ends.

It has been attributed to Kate Smith, an actual "fat lady," who was a popular singer in the 1930s. Irving Berlin wrote "God Bless America" for her. She had her own TV show in the 1950s. It was the last show of the evening before the station went off the air for the night. The TV broadcast day ended when this "fat lady" sang her closing song.[1]

It was also attributed to the sportswriter and broadcaster, Dan Cook. He used the expression "the opera ain't over 'til the fat lady sings," on the air as a way to cheer up the fans in a basketball game.[2]

Bullets Coach Dick Motta liked the saying and used this inspirational message to motivate his own team.

IT'S NOT OVER YET

I WAS GIVEN THE GIFT OF life on Father's Day, June 17th, in the 1930s. When I look back over the years, I realize how blessed I am.

Erma Bombeck wrote, *If Life Is a Bowl of Cherries, What Am I Doing in the Pits?* Her humor had great truths. There exists for all of us the sweet and the sour; try avoiding the pits.

Take advantage of every good trait, every gift you were born with . . . and use it. From a great sense of humor, to a compassionate spirit, to an ability for academics, sports or the arts, etc.—let it shine! The world will notice, and you will reap the rewards.

From the day you enter this world you are presented with a giant puzzle to put together as you grow. This "puzzle of life" is slowly assembled by the choices you make. Some pieces fit together perfectly; sometimes there are pieces that *seem* to fit, but then you realize they are not the right ones. You continue searching for just the right piece.

The puzzle expands as you live your life. More pieces come together in a perfect fit; others remain off to the side as you continue your search for just the right piece to complete your puzzle.

But the missing pieces for completion of your puzzle sometimes seem to elude your searching mind and heart. Eventually, if you are fortunate, you can complete your puzzle before your time is over.

Equating life to a puzzle may seem inane, but I believe we put the pieces together a little each day, without realizing that we are doing it. Choices are nothing more than parts of the "big picture puzzle" we strive to finish as we live our lives.

Edit your life. Get rid of all the unnecessary emotional burdens you place upon yourself.

I often ask myself, "What have I learned from what I have lived?" And I am still learning. Here are some of the important things I often reflect upon.

1. Surround yourself with people you love.
2. There are no free passes in life.
3. Seek humor. Learn to laugh at yourself; it often puts things in a different perspective.
4. Never make a promise you can't keep.
5. Stop striving for perfection. In God's eyes you are perfect. Just strive to do your best.
6. Believe in yourself; it's never too late to do something you love.
7. Never, never give up, and never say never.
8. No one is immune to worries, problems and heartaches in one's lifetime.
9. "Live each day as if it were your last." (I'm not sure who said it . . . but I love it. It appears to be a quote attributed to Jeremy Schwartz. Thanks!)
10. Hold your head high and walk young.
11. "Having somewhere to go is home, having someone to love is family, having both is a blessing." –anonymous
12. Talk to yourself out loud. Ask questions; some of the responses may amaze you.
13. A dear friend once told me the definition of luck is the crossroad between opportunity and preparedness. When you reach it, you had better be ready.
14. To be unaware of the feelings of those around you, be it family or friends, is to be insensitive. Be aware; be sensitive.
15. Two of my mother's favorites:
    a. If everyone hung their troubles on the line, you would take down your own.
    b. Laugh and the world laughs with you. Cry and you cry alone. (The original quote is unknown. It's believed to be a spinoff from "Solitude" by Ella Wheeler Wilcox.)
16. One must bend with the winds of life to remain unbroken.

17. Most of all, stay close to God.

These are some of my favorite quotes from those wiser than me.

"Every day do something that will inch you closer to a better tomorrow."
   —Doug Firebough

"It is never too late to be what you might have been."
   —George Eliot

"Unity tells us the spiritual law of cause and effect is, 'As we think, so we are.'"

"Things do not change; we change."
   —Henry David Thoreau

"We can't take credit for our talents. It's how we use them that counts."
   —Madeleine L'Engle

"Even though I walk through the darkest valley, I fear no evil; for you are with me."
   —My favorite Bible quote (Psalm 23:4)

Leave behind all regrets . . . that which you didn't accomplish and the things you're sorry for. Pack up all your accomplishments and the good you have done and continue on your journey. Regrets belong to the past. They have no place in the present or the future.

My life has been filled with love, but romance was the icing on the cake. Romance is an exhilarating scent and I shall continue to wear it; it is the perfume of my soul.

I feel love is in the air again . . . but, that's another story.

Life is a full spectrum from beginning to end, and *It's Not Over Yet.*

I BELIEVE THAT MY LOVE of storytelling and writing for children began with the story I told for my daughter, Tina. The enthusiastic reception I received from my own children, grandchildren, school children and the young patients in the hospital urged me on. I love to tell a story!

PRINCESS TINA'S TUMMY-ACHE

In the land of the Crystal Palace, nestled at the foot of the Purple Mountains, lived a sweet, even-tempered, young princess. The Queen mother named her Tina, after the first princess of the land, who lived three hundred years earlier.

On the morning of the princess' birth, a family of hummingbirds built their nest in a huge oak tree, just outside the nursery window. They hummed and chirped their lively tunes. They sang the princess to sleep each night and gently woke her in the morning.

She was loved by all. The servants enjoyed teaching her simple songs. "Humm . . . humm," sang the hummingbirds from her windowsill, as they joined Tina's lovely voice each morning.

None of the kings and queens of the surrounding kingdoms were as fortunate to have such a child. The king and queen were very happy—UNTIL . . .

One cold morning, the queen, listening for one of Tina's wake-up songs, heard only silence. Even the hummingbirds were quiet. The queen, thinking the little princess must still be sleeping, went about her daily duties.

When noon arrived, and still no song was heard, the queen decided to see if all was well. Tiptoeing into the princess' room she found her awake. Tears filled Tina's big blue eyes and trickled down her round pink cheeks. Her golden hair stuck to her wet face like glue.

"Oh, Mommy," said the princess, "I have a tummy-ache!" The queen gently soothed her daughter, and then summoned the court's physician.

"Say a-a-ah," said the doctor, looking into her throat. Then he peeked into her ears, her nose, and then her eyes. Finally, he listened to her chest and then her tummy. "Ah hah!" said the doctor. "I hear bubbles in your tummy."

"What could it be?" asked the queen.

"Bubbles . . . bubbles!" repeated the doctor. "I am prescribing a large bowl of oatmeal porridge, each morning, for breakfast."

"I hate porridge!" yelled Princess Tina.

The doctor continued. "The porridge, like a sponge, will soak up all the bubbles. Then, your tummy-ache will be gone."

Immediately, the queen summoned the first cook of the castle. "You will make a tasty oatmeal porridge for the princess."

The porridge arrived on a fine silver tray. The princess took a spoonful. She spit out the porridge and dumped it on her pink satin bed sheets. She screamed, "It's horrible! Get out! Get out!"

The queen was upset and dismissed the first cook. Then, she called upon the second cook and gave her the same instructions. "Please . . . try to make the porridge tasty. The princess must eat it."

Once again, Tina spit out the first spoonful and threw the bowl against the wall. The horrible, gloppy mess slithered down her pink silk walls. "I hate it! I won't eat it! Even the wall doesn't like it!"

The unhappy queen tried to hold back her tears. "Please . . . Tina. Don't be stubborn. Try to eat a little so you will feel better." But, the princess refused.

The queen decided to try one more time. She sent for the third cook and repeated her instructions.

Now, the princess was angry. She threw the bowl of porridge in the third cook's face. "Haa . . . ha, ha, ha, ha," laughed the hysterical princess. The queen watched in horror as the cook tried to wipe the mess from her eyes and ran screaming from the room. The birds, watching from the windowsill, twittered with excitement at the funny scene.

The princess continued to awake each morning with a tummy-ache. None of the cooks were able to please her. She became ill tempered and naughty. She whined and cried when she awoke, no longer singing her lovely songs. Even the hummingbirds stopped singing their tunes.

"What shall we do to make our daughter well again?" cried the queen to the king. "If only someone could cook a porridge she would eat, she would be better in no time at all."

The king thought and thought. Then he said, "We shall offer a reward of one hundred gold pieces to anyone in the kingdom that can make an oatmeal porridge the princess will eat."

The very next day, word of the king's offer spread throughout the kingdom. Cooks arrived at the castle from towns and villages from far and wide. Court jesters, with their silly antics, tried entertaining the princess into eating some porridge. But, no one could make a porridge to please the princess.

One morning, a woman appeared at the door of the kitchen. Her plump figure was dressed in a colorful garment of green, purple, and orange stripes. She had bright red hair fashioned in little curls. Her round, rouged cheeks shone like polished apples. Her green eyes twinkled, and she wore an inviting smile.

"I heard about the unhappy little princess as I was passing through the village," said the woman. "I thought, perhaps, I might try my special recipe. I've cured many a tummy-ache with this one."

The queen looked into the kind eyes of the smiling woman and felt, at once, lighthearted and hopeful. "Please come in," said the queen. "You're welcome to try."

First, the pleasant-faced woman asked for some sweet apples, which she began to cook—till they were just soft. Then, she added some cinnamon, a little cream, a touch of sugar and the very best oatmeal to be had. She cooked the oatmeal, then mashed the soft apples and mixed everything together. When it was finished, she glanced quickly about the kitchen, reached into her pocket, and sprinkled something into the porridge—which made it glow, as if star-dust had been added. The wonderful aroma of the apples filled the castle.

Carrying the small bowl of porridge, she entered the princess' room. Tina stopped crying.

"I see you have visitors," said the woman, referring to the hummingbirds watching from the windowsill. "Perhaps, they might enjoy sharing breakfast with you." She placed a few spoonfuls of the oatmeal porridge on the sill. The birds began pecking at the sweet-smelling porridge, and, in less than a minute, finished it completely. Tina's eyes widened in amazement.

The woman smiled at the little princess and sat down on the edge of her bed. Speaking very softly, she raised a spoonful to the little girl's mouth. To the queen's surprise, the princess swallowed the porridge. In minutes, she had finished the entire bowl.

"I love this porridge," said the princess. "May I have more?"

The queen sighed and beamed with delight. "How did you do it?" she asked.

"Ohh . . . just a bit of magic," replied the woman, as she winked at the princess.

The queen asked the kind woman to remain in the castle and become first cook.

As each day passed, the little princess awoke feeling better and better, until one morning a lovely song could be heard from her room. The hummingbirds flitted back and forth with excitement and joined their little friend in her wake-up song. "Humm . . . humm . . . humm," they joyfully sang.

The king and queen were the happiest parents in the kingdom. Their daughter was well, and once again, was their sweet, even-tempered child,

Every morning thereafter, the king and queen and the family of hummingbirds joined Princess Tina for breakfast. And they all ate the wonderful, magical, oatmeal porridge.

*Live and enjoy today
for
Tomorrow comes without a
Guarantee*

ENDNOTES

PART I: THE EARLY YEARS—**A GRATEFUL SMILE**
[1] http://en.wikipedia.org/wiki/Smile_(Charlie_Chaplin_song)
[2] Ibid.
[3] Ibid.
[4] Ibid.

PART II: THE MIDDLE YEARS & BEYOND—**ISRAEL REVISITED**
[1] http://en.wikipedia.org/wiki/Raoul_Wallenberg
[2] Ibid.
[3] Ibid.

PART II: THE MIDDLE YEARS & BEYOND—**1989: THE SAN FRANCISCO EARTHQUAKE**
[1] http://en.wikipedia.org/wiki/1989_San_Francisco_earthquake

PART III: THE TRAVELLING YEARS—**CRUISE MANIA**
[1] http://en.wikipedia.org/wiki/Lech_Wałęsa
[2] Ibid.

PART III: THE TRAVELLING YEARS—**TRAVEL: THE PASSION CONTINUES**
[1] http://en.wikipedia.org/wiki/Bruges
[2] http://en.wikipedia.org/wiki/William_Wordsworth
[3] http://en.wikipedia.org/wiki/Edinburgh
[4] Ibid.
[5] Ibid.

PART IV: IT'S NOT OVER YET YEARS—**FOREVER FRIENDS: TRAVELLING THROUGH LIFE**
[1] http://www.siegfrieds-musikkabinett.de/
[2] http://en.wikipedia.org/wiki/Wieliczka_salt_mine

PART IV: IT'S NOT OVER YET YEARS—**IT'S NOT OVER YET**
[1] http://en.wikipedia.org/wiki/Kate_Smith
[2] http://en.wikipedia.org/wiki/Dan_Cook

CPSIA information can be obtained at www.ICGtesting.com
Printed in the USA
LVOW010710130213

319875LV00010B/28/P